I0411127

TIMELESS

WRITINGS

#26

A COMPILATION
FOR MANY WRITERS

TATAY JOBO ELIZES
COMPILER, OCTOBER 2016

Published: October 2016

Self-Publisher/Compiler/Printer

Tatay Jobo Elizes, *born 1934 in Manila, now senior ctizen in Brooklyn, NY. Besides self-publishing, he is busy in piglets dispersal programs for livelihood projects in the Philippines.*

.

Acknowledgement

Gratitude and acknowledgment belongs to all contributing writers who gave their permission to compile all articles in a book like this to record history based on timely events that directly or indirectly affect our lives. Copyrights of each article belong to the particular author and he/she is free to re-publish anywhere, without any restriction.

Dedication

I dedicate this book to **all Filipinos** all over the world and to my immediate family, friends and relatives.

This book has the following ISBN numbers:
ISBN-13: 978 - 1539176077
& ISBN-10: 153917607X

Disclaimer:

Views are expressed by the authors alone. Tatay Jobo Elizes does not knowingly publish false information or commit copyright infringement having been given explicit permission to publish this book. Tatay Jobo Elizes may not be held liable for the views of the author exercising his/her right to free expression.

Free pdf file

FREE reading as ebook is available to interested parties. Just email me at **job_elizes@yahoo.com.**

Booklist Websites
http.//tinyurl.com/mj76ccq
www.jobelizes6.wix.com/mysit

Contents

1.
Part I EXECUTIVE SUMMARY---PROBLEMS AND SOLUTIONS IN THE POWER INDUSTRY
(5th Email)

Marcelo L. Tecson

Dateline, August 13, 2016

EXCERPT from the book manuscript entitled PRIVATIZATI ON:

The Fallacious Economic Wisdom EXECUTIVE SUMMARY PROBLEMS AND SOLUTIONS IN THE POWER INDUSTRY STATEMENT OF THE PROBLEM:

ABNORMALLY HIGH POWER RATES COMPOUNDED BY LACK OF AMPLE POWER SUPPLY UNDER EPIRA.

The Electric Power Industry Reform Act (EPIRA) was enacted in 2001 to address our problem of rising power rates. To attain power rate reduction, it tried to foster free-market competition by privatizing and deregulating the power generation phase of the power industry, out of which evolved oligopolistic power generation companies. Under EPIRA, the power generation industry is not only privatized and deregulated, worse, the government is prohibited from engaging in power generation. Thus, even if the private sector does not build power plants on a timely basis, thereby failing to meet growing power demand and needed replacement of aging plants, the government cannot build power plants to prevent any looming supply shortfall. It has to wait first for an impending supply shortage before it can go to Congress to ask for temporary special powers for addressing the emergency. If Congress is dominated by opposition political parties that are hostile to the incumbent Administration, it can hold hostage the granting of emergency powers in order to intentionally have the Administration fail— for political advantage of the opposition parties, at the expense of consumers and the entire economy. Certainly, this set up is inimical to the best interest of Filipinos. Unfortuna tely, EPIRA has miserably failed to live up to its billing as promoter of COMPETITION and consequent low power rates in its privatized and deregulated power generation oligopoly. On the contrary, it gave rise to our highest power rates in the region, compounded by lack of comfortable reserved power generation capacity. Consequently, the nation has faced recurring looming power supply shortfall from scheduled and unscheduled shutdown of aging power plants that can wreak havoc in the economy and discourage local and foreign investors.

ROOTS OF HIGH POWER RATES: FIRST AND FOREMOST, DEREGULATION WITHOUT COMPETITION IN THE POWER GENERATION OLIGOPOLY

Our highest power rates in the region are rooted from a confluence of conditions and events stimulated by EPIRA, such as the following:

1. EPIRA deregulated the privatized power generation oligopoly that evolved under it, on the assumption that free-market COMPETITION by private investors in power generation will emerge and bring about low power rates; the assumed COMPETITION did not materialize—and cannot materialize—in the deregulated and privatized power generation industry because it does not possess the attributes of perfect competition in a real free market, as treated in detail in Chapter III; consequently, higher power rates ensued from LACK of both REGULATION and COMPETITION in power generation. EPIRA is founded on the simplistic free-market assumption that private ownership and deregulation of business equate to competition and low prices. This may be true in real free market for ordinary goods and services, but not in captive markets for basic necessities like power and water. Human nature—within satiable greed for profits as symbolized by profit maximization of business to the extent the market can bear, coupled with opportunity for overpricing in the EPIRA-deregulated power generation oligopoly serving the captive power market, which lacks ample power supply—rendered impossible the emergence of the taken-for-granted competition in power generation.

2. In the case of monopolies in power distribution or marketing in the captive power market clothed with public interest, which have remained regulated under EPIRA pursuant to Section 19, Article XII of the Constitution, there has been improper and deficient regulation by the government.   In power marketing, the Energy Regulatory Commission (ERC) has failed to enforce the Supreme Court ruling that the reasonable return to public utilities like Meralco is 12 percent (ERB vs. Meralco, G.R. No. 141314, November 15, 2002; LAMP et alvs. Meralco, G.R. No. 141369, November 15, 2002).   The Department of Energy (DOE), which is also a Meralco power consumer, has failed in turn to petition ERC to enforce the cited Supreme Court ruling.

As a result, based on its annual reports posted to the Internet, Meralco's actual return on equity (ROE) was 25% in 2012, then 23% in 2013 and 2014, or roughly double what is allowed in existing jurisprudence.

3. With 100% privatization of government assets and operations in the power industry, the government has lost the opportunity to perform its role as instrument of power rate reduction in power generation and marketing.   Among other things, under EPIRA the government cannot own and operate power plants the output of which it can sell at break-even rate—or just a little above it—as means of reducing power rates, similar to what is being done in other countries, as exemplified by the US government's Bonneville Power Administration in Portland, Oregon and Seattle City

Light in Washington, where I had orientation as part of my foreign training years ago.

4. EPIRA could have simply allowed and encouraged private investors to go into power generation together with the government-owned NAPOCOR under a deregulated regime, but it did not—it prohibited instead the government from building and operating power plants, thereby depriving it of its role as catalyst of new investments in power generation, causing lack of ample power supply that contributes to high power rates. EPIRA in effect prohibited NAPOCOR or the government from owning and operating power plants. Hence, even when prospective private investors are discouraged from building new power plants, so that growing power demand out strips total supply, the government still cannot initiate the timely building of new power plants. This situation spawned lack of comfortable reserved power generation capacity whenever there are emergency shutdowns of power plants, especially the aging ones. New power investors are discouraged from building new power plants because of lack of assured market. Retail marketing is under the stranglehold of power marketing monopolies like Meralco. They may have been giving preferential treatment to their power-generation- company affiliates, to the disadvantage of new investors whose entry in power generation may not be welcome because they are future competitors of existing investors.

DEBUNKING THE MYTH OF COMPETITION UNDER EPIRA

There is Simply NO COMPETITION in Meralco's Source of 95% Power Supply—Bilateral

Supply Contracts—as well as in its Source of Remaining 5% Power Supply from WESM,

Here's Why As things currently stand, the EPIRA-provided wholesale electricity spot market (WESM) is a seeming grand deception foisted on Filipino power consumers. It creates the false impression that through it, there is free market competition in the deregulated power generation oligopoly. In reality, as admitted and advertised by Meralco itself (Meralco Advisory, Philippine Daily Inquirer, April 22, 2014, page B3), it sources only a measly 5% power supply from WESM. Its lopsidedly larger 95%power supply is procured through bilateral contracts awarded to power generators without competitive bidding, therefore without competition! The lack of perfect competition in WESM—stemming from lack of enough power supply traded in it because bulk of power generation is already committed to power marketers under bilateral supply contracts—is compounded by the monumentally flawed WESM bidding system. As presented at length in Chapter III, the WESM bidding scheme is actually a game of chance. Under it, whichever happens to be the accepted highest price in the particular batch of rate quotations becomes the winning bid price— even if it is the highest bid rate and there are lower bids received. How this bidding scheme that defies logic and common sense came about is certainly puzzling. Absence of arms-length nature of transaction owing to CONFLICT OF INTEREST is also quite possible in bilateral supply contracts negotiated between Meralco and affiliated power generation companies, or those where it and its major stockholders have some interest or ownership. In this case, Meralco will not be penalized even if higher rates were contracted because under the existing system that evolved under EPIRA, it will simply pass on the higher rates to power consumers. On the contrary, Meralco will gain from the contracted higher rates by way of higher profits by its suppliers, the affiliated power generation companies where it has interest or part ownership.

EXCERPT FROM CHAPTER III:

Meralco's Own Lawyer Exposed Before the Supreme Court the Lackof Price-Lowering Competition in WESM:

He in Effect Admitted that in its Bidding System, Even if there are Submitted Bids at LOWER Rates, these are Deliberately Disregarded and the Accepted HIGHEST Price is Chosen as WINNING Bid Rate—Just What Convoluted Logic Justified this Inanity?

"In the WESM, the sellers of electricity are not paid what they ask for; they are paid what the last accepted bidder asks for. Their bids are arranged from lowest to highest, and the highest accepted price is what is paid by the consumers. So if the maximum bid of P62/kWh is the clearing price, think of the price spike for the consumers and the windfall profits for some power generators." (Solita Collas-Monsod, "Get Real: Who's responsible forpower price spike?" Philippine Daily Inquirer, December 14, 2013,page A12).

Economist Solita Monsod's revelation in her newspaper column of the lack of competition in WESM may not have automatic evidentiary value before our courts, but it was corroborated, admitted, and exposed by Meralco's own lawyer during oral arguments before the Supreme Court, on the petition for temporary restraining order (TRO) against Meralco's P4.15 per kWh rate increase, as follows:

"Senior Associate Justice Antonio Carpio repeatedly asked how many times Meralco had to buy at P62. (Meralco lawyer Victor) Lazatin stressed no buyer can predict the price; given the mechanics, a buyer only states the quantity it needs and Meralco was a price taker. He further said the 'must offer' rule should cover only power not presold, and the price passed to consumers should be each generator's actual quote instead of the highest accepted price. This, he argued, would make quotes realistic, unlike an extreme zero or P62." (Oscar Franklin Tan, "SC proving wrong place for Meralco case," Philippine Daily Inquirer, February 7, 2014, page A12) Thus, even Meralco's own lawyer in effect declared that the WESM winning bid rate should be the actual lowest bid price, instead of the highest accepted price, an indirect admission that the P4.15 per kWh Meralco rate increase, corresponding to the WESM winning bid at HIGHEST accepted price, is NOT right, because what is right is the submitted actual LOWEST bid price....

CAUSES OF EPIRA'S FAILURE TO BRING DOWN ULTRA HIGH POWER RATES

Here is a summary of the apparent causes of EPIRA's failure to bring down our ultra high power rates, treated in Part III of Chapter II.

1. The EPIRA-mandated 100% privatization of the government-owned power-generator monopoly—National Power Corporation

(NAPOCOR)—caused the government to abdicate its role as instrument of rate reduction and catalyst of new investments in the captive power market clothed with public interest. Under EPIRA, the government cannot build power plants even if there is imminent shortage in power generation capacity, resulting from the inability of discouraged private investors to build new plants on a timely basis. New plants are needed in meeting growing power demand and in replacing aging plants. New power generation investors are discouraged from building new plants owing to lack of assured market. The retail power market is under the stranglehold of monopolistic power marketers, like Meralco, which give preferential patronage and better terms to their affiliated power generation companies.

Under the same law, the government cannot own and operate power plants the output of which it can sell at break-even rate—or just a little above it— to reduce power rates.

2. The EPIRA-mandated deregulation of the power generation oligopoly, which replaced the government-owned NAPOCOR as builder and operator of power plants, did not—and cannot— produce the expected COMPETITION in the deregulated power generation industry. To show the utter lack of competition among deregulated power generators, in the case of Meralco, 95% of its power supply is sourced through bilateral contracts, awarded to power generation companies on negotiated basis and without competitive bidding, hence devoid of competition.

There is also no true competition in Meralco's remaining 5% supply sourced through the wholesale electricity spot market (WESM) created under EPIRA. Its inane bidding scheme is merely a game of chance. Under it, whichever is the accepted highest price in the particular batch of bids—even if there are much lower bids received—becomes the winning bid price. Here then is a ridiculous and appalling case of awarding purchase transactions on the basis of highest and most disadvantageous bid!

3.   Unlike the MWSS Charter(RA 6234) which set 12% rate-of-return ceiling on water companies, as well as the Build-Operate- Transfer (BOT) Law (RA 6957 as amended by RA 7718) which imposed 12% as return limit under certain conditions, EPIRA failed to prescribe 12% return ceiling on power companies, resulting in deficient regulation of still regulated power marketers like Meralco, with concomitant high power rates. It is astounding how economic and financial experts in and out of government have missed a crucial point in rate regulation—the need to institute control or safety net against unreasonable rates. That control mechanism is the reasonable return ceiling which should be competitive to private investors' opportunity cost. As treated in Chapter II and as ruled by the Supreme Court, 12% is the reasonable return to public service providers like Meralco (ERB vs. Meralco, G.R. No. 141314,November 15, 2002).

4.   EPIRA provided theexcuse for ERC's implementation of fallacious performance-based regulation (PBR) that produced much higher power rates, in violation of Meralco's own franchise (RA 9209), which mandates it to "supply electricity to its captive market in the least cost manner...." With Meralco's 25% return on equity in 2012 and 23%

thereafter based on its annual reports posted to its website—more than double the cited 12% reasonable return ruled for it by the Supreme Court—Meralco is definitely not charging its captive market in the least cost manner. The apparent root of its breaching the Supreme-Court ruled 12% reasonable return limit is ERC's implementation of fallacious performance based regulation (PBR).

 The ERC-implemented   PBR for Meralco is fallacious because it results in consumers' DOUBLE PAYMENT on increase in rates for future capital investments and asset revaluation. There is double payment because PBR entails DOUBLE BILLING to power consumers, directly traceable to lack of skill in ACCOUNTING by those responsible for PBR. The increase in rate for future capital projects and asset revaluation is lumped with regular electricity rate and treated as income of MERALCO. Hence, the cumulative rate increase is recorded in Meralco's books of accounts as retained earnings, the income plowed back into business that forms part of stockholders' equity or capital invested by stockholders. As a result, once the accumulated rate increase is actually spent in capital projects, upon project completion, it will be treated as assets owned and invested by stockholders, subject again to recovery as annual depreciation and rate of return from victimized unsuspecting consumers, otherwise Meralco will not attain its 12% allowablerate of return.

What's more, increasing power rates on account of future capital expenditures shifts the funding responsibility from Meralco to consumers. This goes against Meralco's representation when it applied for franchise that it is financially capable to perform the obligations of a franchise holder, otherwise its application should not have been approved.

SUMMARY OF NEEDED CRUCIAL REFORMS IN THE POWER INDUSTRY

PART I REFORMS THAT CAN BE INSTITUTED WITHOUT AMENDMENT OF EXISTING LAWS

Proper REGULATION of the Power DISTRIBUTION Industry Pursuant to Section 19,Article XII of the Constitution, the government should religiously and consistently rein in within reasonable range the service rates of monopolies in captive markets clothed with public interest.

1. Enforcement by the Energy Regulatory Commission (ERC) ofthe 12% ROE ceiling on Meralco and other regulated power distributors to attain Supreme- Court ruled reasonable return to investors at reasonable rates to consumers. Under the constitutional protection against monopolies in captive markets imbued with public interest, there is a long standing Supreme Court ruling that 12% is the reasonable rate of return for Meralco and other public utilities. [ERB vs. Meralco, G.R. No.141314, November 15, 2002; Manila Electric Company v. Public Service Commission, 18 SCRA 651, 665-666 (1966)] This means that this 12% reasonable return should not be exceeded by them, otherwise the results will be unreasonable return to investors and unreasonable rates to consumers. Consequently, the Supreme-Court ruled 12% reasonable return equates to 12% rate-of-return ceiling for monopolistic public utility companies.

Based on Meralco's financial reports posted to the Internet, its actual return on equity (ROE) was 25% in 2012, then 23% from 2013 to 2015, hence it had already breached and violated the Supreme Court decision on 12% reasonable return to public utilities. Prompt implementation of this profit-rate ceiling will reduce our present highest power rates, through bringing down to 12% reasonable return level all actual rates of return in excess of it.

2. After ERC has brought down Meralco's and other power marketers' rates to the equivalent of 12%reasonable return, any further rate increase should be for cost-increase recovery only, otherwise they will breach anew the 12% return limit. After ERC has set power rates at 12% reasonable return, any future rate increase should be for cost-increase recovery only, otherwise any further rate increase in excess of cost recovery will produce higher net income and ROE in breach of the 12% ROE ceiling. (Reference: Chapter I). This means that tightness in supply owing to shutdowns of some power plants is not aground for rate increase by remaining operating plants, because they do not incur any cost increase from the shutdowns of other plants.

3. While EPIRA is not yet overhauled, institution by ERCand DOE of drastic reforms In WESM bidding rules to inject reason into the present senseless bidding system. ERC and DOE should promptly revoke the Wholesale Electricity Spot Market (WESM) bidding rules authorized by their officials in the past—because as a system that awards purchase transactions to higher or even highest bid rates despite the availability of low and

even zero bid rates, it is not only a mockery of government bidding rules that award purchase transactions to lowest price bidders, it is also the means of victimizing through unreasonably high power rates not only millions of private consumers in households and business, but also government agencies and entities that meekly buy overpriced electricity from Meralco, like Malacanang, ERC, DOE, COA, Office of the Ombudsman, etc. (Reference: Chapter III). The Use of Single Price CAP in WESM Bid Rates Can be High for Low-Cost Hydro and Geothermal Power Plants and Low for High-Cost Coal- and Oil-fired Plants

To quote from a news report: "DOE, ERC tackle parameters of secondary WESM cap," by Iris Gonzales, The Philippine Star Online, October2 , 2014: "In May, the ERC imposed a secondary price cap of P6.245 per kilowatt-hour at the Wholesale Electricit y Spot Market (WESM), the country's trading floor for electricity, and extended this indefinitely. "The ERC has extended the secondary price cap indefinitely or until a permanent measure is in place....Power generators have said the price cap is too low but the ERC said the amount has taken into account the need for power producers to recover their costs. Still, (Energy secretary) Petilla said the parameters in implementing the cap may be too low. 'It exists in other countries but the parameters must not be biased against diesel plants so the ERC can change the parameters. Merchant plants must be allowed to recover their costs,' he said. Merchant plants are facilities that do not have power supply contracts." The use of a single price cap—applied to contrasting conditions: low and high power generation costs per kWh—in the present WESM bidding rules is the source of unfairness and controversy on the proper amount of the price cap. The single amount is low and unfair for high-cost power plants, like coal- and oil-fired plants, and unduly high for low-cost power generators, like hydro and geothermal plants, hence unfair to consumers.

Suggested SOLUTION: Setting Separate Price Cap in WESM Bid Rates, Tailor-Made for Each Type of Power Plant with Unique Generation Cost Per kWh, to be Done in Effect on Specific Identification or Case to Case Basis Per Type of Plant

As the WESM bidding can be participated in by both low-cost and high-cost power generators—and we cannot do away with the high-cost generators because their power supply is needed in meeting total demand—it is unfair to apply as winning bid the possible lowest offer of low-cost generators to the offered supply at higher rates by high-cost generator-bidders—because while the former can already earn reasonable return on their lowest offer, the high-cost producers can be marginally earning or even losing from it. This unfair situation is untenable because low-cost generators cannot supply the total market demand, so we have to live with the high-cost generators, but we have to give them the needed reasonable return through higher winning bid rates. Or else, they will get out of power generation and cause bigger supply shortfall, with dire consequences. On the other hand, it is also not right to have the low-cost generators enjoy the higher rates for high-cost producers, because—at the expense of hapless consumers—the former will gain rate of return in excess of what is reasonable as already quantified by the Supreme Court (ERB vs. Meralco, G.R.No. 141314, November 15, 2002). The solution then is to set separate price cap in WESM bid rates, based on each type of power plant with unique generation cost per kWh depending on power generation process or feedstock.

4. ERC should similarly prescribe separate PRICE CAP per type of power plant for the now 95% power supply to Meralco under bilateral supply contracts, as well as for power supply to similarly situated power retailers. For greater protection of consumers, the setting of PRICE CAP for each typeof power generation should be similarly applied to power supply to Meralco and other power marketers under bilateral supply contracts, which pass through ERC for prior review and approval.

5. ERC should require the regulated monopoly MERALCO to conduct genuine competitive bidding on its wholesale power purchases, as basis of its awarding of bilateral supply contracts for its now 95% power supply emanating from deregulated power producers—not from WESM—otherwise ERC should not approve any excessive power GENERATION charge as Meralco's PASS ON charge to power consumers; ERC should apply the same measure to similarly situated monopolistic power retailers in other franchise areas. At the soonest opportunity, such as in Meralco's entering into new bilateral supply contracts or renewal of existing contracts with power generators, ERC should require MERALCO to conduct competitive bidding

as precondition to and basis of the power marketer's awarding of supply contracts to deregulated power generation companies, otherwise Meralco's contracted rates will not be honored by ERC and will not be approved as PASS ON charge to power consumers.   It may not be within ERC's power to impose conditions on the deregulated oligopolistic power producers, but it is within its power to impose conditions (like prior competitive bidding on bilateral supply contracts) on the regulated monopoly Meralco. It is within Meralco' s prerogative in turn to conduct competitive bidding as precondition to its award of supply contracts to power generators, not only as required by ERC but also as part of usual best management practices by private corporations on their procurement of goods and services.

On February 9, 2015, I emailed to DOE Secretary Carlos Jericho Petilla and other high government officials some recommended doable solutions to high power rates, including prior competitive bidding in awarding of power distributors' bilateral supply contracts. I followed it up with my May 26, 2015 letter personally transmitted to DOE on June 3, 2015. Before resigning as DOE secretary, Secretary Petilla issued DOE Circular No. DC 2015-06-0008 dated June11, 2015, which prescribed public bidding in awarding of bilateral supply contracts. It was subsequently affirmed in the implementing rules issued by ERC. As it turned out, ERC's move to implement the bidding requirement "comes after a period of study and consultation with concerned industry players and stakeholders of over two years" (Riza T. Olchondra, "Bidding ordered for power utilities' supply deals," Philippine Daily Inquirer, November 7, 2015, page B3). Why ERC took its own sweet time in deciding on something so basic, crucial, and clear cut suggests regulatory capture. It was only after DOE jumped the gun on ERC through the cited DOE circular that ERC, under a new Chairman, was constrained to follow suit and issued its own affirming implementing rules.

6. Overhauling of fallacious Performance Based Regulation (PBR) inregulated retail marketer Meralco; the PBR entails double billing on future investments and asset replacement values erroneously built into existing power rates; the double billing is a product of lack of expertise in accounting by those responsible for the PBR. As previously presented herein in no. 4 of Causes of EPIRA's Failure to Bring Down Ultra High Power Rates, there is DOUBLE BILLING under PBR on unwarranted inclusion of future investments and asset replacement values in present power rates. The double billing is discernible by accountants but perhaps not by economists without adequate accounting background. The appropriate performance based regulation that should be applied to Meralco is an ERC-set diminishing schedule of system loss chargeable to consumers until the loss reaches zero level. If Meralco will attain it, fine, it will be rewarded through reduced losses. If not, it will be penalized through shouldering the cost of unattained loss reduction as it should be no longer chargeable to consumers. It should not be included either as deductible expense in the determination of net income subject to the 12% reasonable return limit.

7. The Department of Energy should monitor the annual ROE of oil companies and issue SUGGESTED RETAIL PRICE (SRP) for each petroleum product as moral deterrent to profiteering. It is not right for the government to let down its guard and simply assume that, with taken-for- granted competition in the deregulated oil industry, it will never indulge in overpricing. As moral deterrent to profiteering, the Department of Energy should monitor the annual return on equity (ROE) of oil companies and issue SUGGESTED RETAIL PRICE (SRP) for each marketed petroleum product, especially diesel and bunker fuel oil which are used as feedstock in power generation. DOE should follow the example of the Department of Trade and Industry (DTI), which issues regularly updated SRP for deregulated key commodities in the market.

8. In any government privatization or awarding of public service project to private investors, the government should always conduct public bidding on lowest project construction cost—this is something basic yet apparently violated in the CALAX bidding held in June 2014 as well as in all other PPP projects so far.

To come up with reasonable rates to the paying public, the government should keep as low as practicable the project investment costs that will be recovered from the public through service rates. To attain this objective, the Procurement Law, RA 9184, has mandated the conduct of public bidding on procurement of all government infrastructure projects, whether or not the projects will be subject to charges to the using public. I am at a loss as to how the Procurement Law (RA

9184)—as well as the Build-Operate-Transfer (BOT) Law (RA 6957 as amended by RA 7718)—can be blatantly violated in big-time government public service projects, where the standard public bidding on lowest construction cost—together with lowest service rates once the projects are operational—is not done. This violation of existing laws, presented in Chapter I, should be stopped by the Office of the President, the Department of Justice, the Commission on Audit (COA), or the Office of the Ombudsman.

9. In government awarding of new public service projects toprivate investors, as well as privatization of its existing assets or operations, the government should conduct public bidding on lowest return on equity (ROE) that the winning bidder is willing to accept during the franchise/concession period or service life of each public service project—because some bidders may accept ROE lower than 12%, as in the case of the media-reported 10% ROE acceptable to Mr. Ramon Ang on his proposed $10-billion airport project. In any government privatization in captive markets affected with public interest, or in any awarding of new public service projects to private monopolies or oligopolies, the government should institute an economic policy that requires public bidding not just on the initial rate but also on future escalated rates. Once existing rates of the winning bidder already equate to its winning lowest bid on percent ROE ceiling, further rate escalation should be for cost recovery only, not for increased profit, otherwise the winning bidder will exceed its committed ROE limit.

To illustrate, the highly defective MWSS privatization scheme in 1997 involved public bidding on initial water rates only. It did not include bidding on lowest ROE ceiling that each bidder is willing to earn during the franchise or concession period, which could have resulted in lowest future escalated rates. Such lack of public bidding on lowest ROE ceiling deprived consumers of safety net against water rate escalation beyond reasonable level, which has actually happened in the case especially of Maynilad. It earned unconscionably high ROE of as much as 247% in 2008 and 147% in 2009, as well as returns higher than 12% ROE in subsequent years. (Reference: Chapter V) Bidding Competition on Lowest Future Escalated Rates Should be in Terms of Lowest Percent ROE Ceiling Acceptable To Private Investor- Bidders. The competition on future escalated rates should NOT be in terms of LOWEST PESO AMOUNT PER UNIT of product or service, because accurately forecasting on long-term basis the proper future service rates in peso amount per unit is not possible at the time of public bidding. The competition during public bidding on future escalated service rates—which will be charged during the concession or franchise period—should be expressed in LOWEST PERCENT RETURN ON EQUITY (ROE) viable and acceptable to each competing bidder, because whatever is the present reasonable percent return on equity—which is higher or better than OPPORTUNITY COST—is a more stable profitability measure that is not likely to require drastic upward adjustment in future years.

Today, to correct past errors in privatization and

awarding of public service projects to private investors, the government should promptly institute bidding on lowest percent ROE at which the winning bidder will operate, because it does not follow that the winner should be allowed the Supreme-Court ruled 12% ROE ceiling. This is just the maximum rate allowable.

10. The Department of Energy (DOE) should review the feed-intariff (FIT) for renewable energy and, if found necessary, coordinate with the Energy Regulatory Commission (ERC) towards the streamlining of the present apparently weak FIT system. The DOE should review the feed-in tariff (FIT) instituted by ERC for renewable energy, like wind and solar. Under the present system, the Meralco power rate already includes a fixed increase for FIT, but it is not clear if this is being collected and accumulated as a buffer fund, which will be used later to satisfy actual claims by renewable energy generators.

In which case, the FIT collection should be treated as a trust fund subject to periodic accounting by Meralco—similar to the government's regular accounting for the Oil Price Stabilization Fund (OPSF) during the oil industry regulation regime that ended in 1998. Otherwise, Meralco may ask for further rate increase if the FIT collection becomes insufficient, or may keep quiet and appropriate for itself any surplus that develops. In other words, control is weak in the present system. As a better alternative, FIT collection from Meralco consumers should be done based on actual sales and claims by operating renewable energy companies, similar to what is being done in WESM where actual increase in winning WESM bid rate is passed on to Meralco as and when incurred.

11. Other recommendations: as proper risk management, taking of exchange rate hedging on foreign obligations of Meralco and other power companies—in lieu of Currency Exchange Rate Adjustment (CERA) and Foreign Currency Differential Adjustment (FCDA)—taking of insurance coverage against fire, earthquake, and typhoon losses instead of loss recovery through rate increase, as well as refund of past over-recoveries on billed peso depreciation after the peso subsequently appreciated and the still unpaid foreign obligations can be paid at the appreciated peso. In any government privatization or awarding of public service project to private investors, the government should not repeat its past errors and failures in public bidding and regulation that resulted in unwarrantedly high service rates to the public, such as those presented in Chapters II and VI, like lack of exchangerate hedging, use of fallacious and hard-to-breach 12% RORB ceiling, faulty currency exchange rate adjustment (CERA) mechanism, grossly defective performance based regulation (PBR), lack of insurance coverage against force majeure or natural calamities, etc.

oo0Ooo

2.

EXECUTIVE SUMMARY---PROBLEMS AND SOLUTIONS IN THE POWER INDUSTRY, Parts II and III (5th Email)

Marcelo L. Tecson

Dateline, August 3, 2016

EXECUTIVE SUMMARY
PART II REFORMS THAT NEED PRIOR LEGISLATION

Reforms in laws other than EPIRA are also needed in captive markets imbued with public interest.

1. Institution of Return on Equity (ROE)—not Return On Rate Base (RORB) as prescribed under Section 12 of the MWSS Charter (RA 6234)—as basis of 12% reasonable return ceiling ruled by the Supreme Court, because using RORB is plain erroneous—something that is discernible by accountants but maybe not by laymen; pertinent laws should be amended accordingly.   Why ROE is the Correct Measure of Profit-Rate Limit for Meralco and Other Public Service Companies Return on equity is the proper measure of profitability of public utilities, like Meralco, because it correctly represents the fact that the rate of return is a measure of profit rate on investment by whoever made the investment—and that investment upon which the return has to be

measured constitutes capital or stockholders' equity in the case of public service corporations, hence the need to measure their profitability as percent return on equity or ROE. In addition, ROE has to be used as profit-rate limit because it is the one that meets the requirement in doing what has to be done from time to time: ERC's determination of the continuing reasonableness or propriety of prevailing power rates, which can be ascertained through looking at the power companies' actual rates of return compared to power investors' opportunity cost—or rate of return foregone from alternative investments not taken when they invested instead in the power industry. If their rates of return compare favorably to opportunity cost—or stay at about the 12% return limit even after incurring some cost increases— then they have no valid reason to ask for any rate increase and ERC should deny their rate increase petition under the circumstances.

Thus, once ERC has enforced on a sustained basis the Supreme-Court ruled 12% rate-of-return ceiling, to justify the government's continuing adherence to it whenever it is under attack by power companies that want astronomical increase in power rates, the continuing reasonableness of the 12% return ceiling has to be tested and compared to power investors' opportunity cost. As the prevalent alternative investments (stocks and bonds, money-market placements, Treasury bills, trust funds, etc. which usually yields less than 12% return) usually do not involve the investors' operation of physical assets in companies where they invested, the foregone rate of return or opportunity cost is expressed as return on invested capital or return on investment (terminologies that apply to both individual and corporate investors), which equates to return on equity (ROE) in the case of corporations, like the power generators and marketers. Hence, for comparability with opportunity cost, ROE should be the measure of allowed rate of return to regulated public service companies. (Reference: Chapter VII) The usual profitability measure used in evaluating the market value of stocks traded in the stock market is price-earnings (P/E) ratio (stock price divided by earnings per share), not ROE. Even then, ROE remains the proper ratio in setting the rate-of-return ceiling of regulated industries.

The resulting stock market price of stocks as purchase price and capital invested by new stockholders consists of the original investment plus profit of the selling stockholders that go to the latter's pockets, not to the funds owned by the regulated companies. There are mere changes in company stockholders from the stock market transactions done privately among old and new stockholders outside the companies. Moreover, the majority stockholders in regulated companies hold their shares as long-term investment for control purposes. They do not normally sell except in case of divestment. Those who usually sell are speculators. If regulated companies with shares traded in the stock market are subject to rate-of-return limit, their P/E ratios will move taking into account this constraint, hence new investors will be guided accordingly in their stock price evaluation.

Why RORB is a Wrong Measure of Profit-Rate Limit and Should Not be Applied to Meralco, Maynilad and Manila Water, as well as Other Public Service Companies RORB, with assets in operation as rate base, is a wrong profitability measure for public service companies in captive markets clothed with public interest, because it is relating net income, accruing to stockholders alone, to assets in operation acquired through funding by both stockholders and creditors—instead of relating the net income to smaller asset amount financed out of stockholders equity only—in the process making the 12% RORB limit impossible to breach unless the service rates are at already ultra high and unreasonable level. In short, the net income accruing to stockholders should be related solely to the EQUITY or funds invested by them and used to acquire part of assets in operation—because the interest income of creditors, whose funds were used to acquire the remaining part of assets in operation, was already set aside and provided to them by way of company interest expense that reduced the net income accruing to corporate stockholders.

Expecting again a 12% return to stockholders, on top of interest income already earned by creditors, on creditor-funded assets in operation will entail double count of income on the creditor-financed assets—first as interest payment to creditors and second as 12% return to stockholders— thereby resulting in high service rates that will crucify victimized consumers. (Reference: Chapter V). Illustrative Example of Monumental Error in Using Retrun on Rate Base (RORB) as Rate-of-Return Ceiling For Public

Service Companies that Use Borrowed Funds Let us assume the following financial data (in Philippine pesos):

Assets in operation (99 funded by loans and 1 by equity) ......100 Liabilities (Loans) .....   99 Equity (Capital) ....   1 Interest on loans (loan balances constant during the year) ..... 11.88 Net income for the year.................... .... 12 The respective returns to creditors and stockholders are as follows:

Rate of return to creditors: Interest payments to creditors, 11.88 over 99 loans 12%

Rates of return to stockholders: RORB: 12 net income over 99 + 1 or 100 assets in operation ..... 12%   ROE: 12 net income over 1 Equity .... 1,200% Analysis of Financial Statistics a. Return to Creditors: The creditors' return on loans used to acquire P99 worth of assets consists of the P11.88 or 12% interest on loans incurred by the company as interest expense, thereby resulting in reduced net income already net of creditors' return on the assets financed by them.

b. Return to Stockholders: For their 12% maximum RORB, with assets used in operation as rate base, corporate stockholders are entitled to P12 net income or 12% return on P100 total assets used in operation. The P12 net income is broken down as follows:

(1) P11.88 or 12% return on the P99 assets financed by creditors, and

(2) P0.12 or 12% return on the P1 asset acquired out of stockholders' capital investment or equity.   Clearly, under fallacious RORB, there is

double reckoning of return on the P99 creditor-financed assets—first, to creditors as P11.88 interest on loans, and second, to stockholders as P11.88 net income even if they were not the ones who funded the acquisition of the P99 assets. The result is pure and simple DOUBLE BILLING to consumers.

In the example, the stockholders will recover within one year 12 times their invested capital or equity, yet they will still NOT EXCEED the prescribed 12% RORB ceiling, exactly the reason why, in the case of Maynilad, despite its unconscionably high rates of return on equity (ROE) of as much as 247% in 2008 and 147% in 2009 based on its annual reports to stockholders, it did not exceed the 12% RORB ceiling imposed by Section 12 of RA 6234 (MWSS Charter) as well as by Article 9, Section 9.1 of the MWSS concession agreement that adopted the 12% RORB limit set by the MWSS Charter.

2. Institution of cap in ad valorem VAT on power and water rates, to prevent the government from profiting from further miseries of consumers from inflationary rise in utility rates. If the government cannot subsidize generally poor power and water consumers, including manufacturers that help promote economic growth, it should, at the very least, not gain from ever increasing power and water rates. At present the government profits from price increases through the corresponding 12% ad valorem VAT on the increase in prices. To avoid such increase in VAT collection from already suffering poor consumers, the government should set a cap on peso-per-unit power and water rates subject to VAT.

The government should not worsen inflation provoked by increase in VAT amount—even without increase in percent VAT rate—as a result of rise in VAT able power and water rates. Unless remedied, we have the present anomalous situation where the government also gains, and adds more hardship to the people, from further rise in utility rates through the ad valorem VAT—and the remedial measure is simple but it needs legislation.

PART III

REFORMS THAT NEED ENABLING EPIRA AMENDMENTS

The government should institute crucial reforms in the power industry through overhauling EPIRA. The reforms can be capsulized as partial reversal of its 100% privatization policy to enable it to effectively perform its role as instrument of power rate reduction and catalyst of new investments in power generation. Under partial privatization, the government will not subsidize power consumers on a continuing basis year after year out of the national budget. It will need seed capital for investment in power plants—which it will recoup by way of depreciation- expense recovery from revenue.

Only its internally generated net profit will be used to reduce power rates—and its rate reduction should be properly viewed as PROFIT DISTRIBUTION—not SUBSIDY—to the benefiting public that owns the government power plants. Once a government power plant is privatized (except low-cost hydro and geothermal plants which should not be privatized because these do not entail corruption-prone huge coal and oil feedstock purchases), the privatization proceeds will be used to build a new plant—and this cycle of exploring for suitable site, building new power plant, and privatizing it once it has enough market from accumulated growth in demand, will continuously go on.

Following is an enumeration of the major reforms needed in addressing ultra high power rates and inadequate power supply in the power sector, expounded on in Part III of Chapter VII. Enabling legislation, in the form of drastic EPIRA amendments, is needed because the reforms are contrary to the existing provisions of EPIRA and, if implemented without changing this law, will become in violation of it.

1. The government should perform its role as instrument of rate reduction in the power industry. Under partial privatization, the government should co-own some power companies, where its share in profits will be waived and used to reduce power rates. For further rate reduction, it should fully own low-cost hydro and geothermal plants—because these are less prone to corruption owing to lack of fertile ground for kickbacks: induced emergency purchases for big-ticket procurement of coal and oil feedstocks in government-owned coal- and oil-fired plants. It should operate at break-even point—no gain, no loss—or slightly above it to enable it to charge lower rates and help attain rate reduction.

2. The government should undertake its role as catalyst of new investments in power generation. To address discouraged investments by new investors in power generation, the government should be allowed to wholly or partly

own and operate power plants, co-own power marketing companies, and pursue the policy of EXPLORE-BUILD- and-PRIVATIZE power plants in the power generation industry, with the government providing bulk of needed plant reserved capacity. Under present EPIRA, reserved capacity is not being provided by private investors because it will mean idle plant capacity and consequent financial loss for them. This is the root of the recurring situation where we have tightness and even looming shortage in power supply. To meet continuing growth in power demand through having power plant construction always ahead of rise in demand, the government should take matter into its hands by taking control of events that will lead to sustained adequate power supply—through EXPLORE-BUILD- and-PRIVATIZE strategy in the power generation industry. Under the suggested strategy, the government will do the following on a continuing cycle:

- Continuously explore suitable new power plant sites.

- Based on projected power demand, build power plants just enough to provide needed comfortable reserved capacity. Defer or slow down the building of new plants If there are private investors planning to definitely build new plants.

c. Maintain at all times the needed reserved capacity.

- As demand grows and one or more reserved plants are now operating to meet the heretofore accumulated growth in demand, privatize wholly or partly the now fully operational new plants. Exclude from privatization low-cost hydro and geothermal plants because the government can operate these without incurring losses as these are not susceptible to corruption. These do not require corruption-prone induced emergency procurement of huge amounts of coal and oil feedstocks in government-owned coal- and oil-fired plants.

It will be much easier for private investors to go to power generation through buying government-privatiz ed power plants with existing enough market share, compared to the extremely difficult and time-consuming process of doing everything—from plant site exploration, securing of government permits, plant construction, and development of enough market share.

- Use the privatization sales proceeds in building replacement new power plants to constantly maintain needed reserved capacity. This way, privatization will not mean mere change in ownership of privatized plants from government to private investors as in the present case under EPIRA, it will also mean increase in national power generation capacity.

With government providing reserved plant capacity and private investors given first crack in serving accumulated growth in power demand under the government's EXPLORE-BUILD- and-PRIVATIZE strategy, it will encourage new economic players and serve as catalyst of new investments in power generation.

3. As part of EPIRA overhaul, the government should be prohibited from entering into take-or-pay contracts with private generation companies as means of addressing the need for reserved capacities—because DOE and ERC

officials and staff have not shown genuine interest, expertise, industriousness, initiative, creativity, and eternal vigilance in protecting power consumers from abuses and overcharging under this scheme. Providing take-or-pay concession—or guaranteed return with or without utilization of plant capacity—to private generation companies for power plant reserved capacity is not advisable because this is susceptible to abuse and overcharging, which is hard to check under deregulation. I have an old Meralco electric bill for the period January 15 to February 14, 2003 (copy attached as ANNEX A) with power purchase adjustment (PPA) for take-or-pay contracts at P2.761 per kWh, which was practically equal to energy consumption charge at P2.7852 per kWh.

The almost equal rates for actual electricity consumption and guaranteed payment for unutilized power plant capacity meant either or both of two things—the total reserve capacity subject to take-or-pay concession was practically equal to total operational capacity, and/or the fixed cost and return on investment to be recovered through the take-or-pay PPA rate   per KWh of the   small total reserved capacity was so astronomically high, both of which were likely not the actual case, hence I suspect overpricing.

The charge for unutilized capacities under take-or-pay contracts might have been illogically high because these erroneously included variable production costs, such as coal or oil feedstock, that were incurred in direct proportion to production by operating power plants, but not by idle ones on their unutilized capacities. In other words, there are so many things to be done to ensure the technical accuracy of take-or-pay rate per kWh which DOE and ERC apparently failed to do in the past.

4. The government should restore REGULATION of the power generation industry, to be implemented the proper and equitable way, under which investors earn reasonable return on their investments while consumers are charged reasonable rates for their power consumption.

The power generation industry is unique. It produces the same kind of product or service—electricity—but the generation processes, feedstocks, and per unit generation costs can vary greatly. While there are low-generation- cost power plants like hydro and geothermal, high-cost plants like coal- and oil-fired ones are a necessary evil because we have limited possible sites for the low-cost plants.

Under the present EPIRA set-up where power generation companies with greatly varying generation costs are supposedly competing in the same tight-supply WESM market, the bid prices will likely unify at higher rather than lower rates. The low-cost generators will simply ride on the high bids of high-cost companies and can still sell at the same high prices—because owing to lack of enough supply, under EPIRA mandated deregulation, the captive power market has no choice but to patronize all offered supplies regardless of price.

Only REGULATION can inject order and fairness into the messy and unfair-to-consumer situation. Under regulation, the market can be made to behave the way it should behave. Power rates can be regulated on specific identification or case to case basis. Rates can be set high for high-cost generators and low for low-cost ones, with all of them earning the corresponding allowable reasonable return on their varying invested capital at equivalent reasonable rates to consumers.

5.   Once EPIRA is amended and REGULATION is restored, the government should institute power rate reduction among power generation companies, up to the point that will yield them reasonable return at reasonable rates to consumers.   As first step in power rate reduction, the government should bring down any excessive power generators' return under deregulation to 12% reasonable level under regulation. Thereafter, any further rate increase will be for cost recovery only, otherwise the 12% return ceiling will be breached.

As second step, the government should waive its share of net income in power companies where it has full or partial ownership and use the same in rate reduction.   IN SUM, WHY EPIRA HAS TO BE OVERHAULED. EPIRA has to be amended to destroy the roots of our present major problems: abnormally high power rates and recurring power supply shortfall. This law provided the nourishment for the vitality and growth of these problems, as in the case of the power-rate-raising ERC-implemented performance- based regulation (PBR), approved through invoking the resort to alternative methodology allowed under EPIRA. PBR was the start of huge profits for Meralco. Why it is technically wrong is presented in Chapter II. By EPIRA's fruit we shall know it. Under the present regime governed by EPIRA, the no. 1 power distributor in the land, the monopoly Meralco, earned 25% return on equity (ROE) in 2012, as shown on page 38 of its submission to the Securities and Exchange Commission (SEC) posted to its website in the Internet. Its ROE thereafter was 23% from 2013 to 2015. Clearly, Meralco's actual rate of return has been roughly double the 12% reasonable return ruled by the Supreme Court in 1966, reiterated in its landmark decision on Meralco's income tax many years later (ERB vs. Meralco, G.R. No. 141314, November 15, 2002), cited in Chapter II.

EPIRA serves as obstacle to our economic progress because while it nurtured the cited problems, it does not allow the corresponding solutions, thereby perpetuating the problems that burden the poor, harm commerce and industry, and impede our industrialization. EPIRA has to be overhauled to restore what it took away since 2001 from the government—the power to curb any overpricing among oligopolistic power generation companies, as well as the authority to build and operate its own power plants—in order to perform its role as instrument of rate reduction and catalyst of investments in power generation. The government's proper exercise of these power and authority—not sitting idly by under unbridled free market—constitutes the solution to our existing price and supply problems in the power industry.

Sincerely,
MARCELO L. TECSON, 4-23-15, 7-26-16

ooo0ooo

3.

HOW TO REDUCE TELECOM, POWER, AND OTHER PUBLIC SERVICE RATES: DO NOT LEAVE EVERYTHING TO ECONOMISTS

(NOTE: In a future email)

Marcelo L. Tecson

Dateline, Sent: Friday, September 16, 2016

Subject: (Revised) WHAT ECONOMISTS NEVER TOLD US: THE ELUSIVE SOLUTION TO HIGH PUBLIC SERVICE RATES

WHAT ECONOMISTS NEVER TOLD US: THE ELUSIVE SOLUTION TO   HIGH PUBLIC SERVICE RATES OBSERVE THAT ALL OF OUR HIGH POWER, WATER, TELECOM, AND TOLL-ROAD RATES ARE ROOTED FROM A COMMON DENOMINATOR: LACK OF ENFORCED SAFETY NET   AGAINST   OVERPRICING: RATE-OF-RETURN LIMIT

THE SOLUTION THEN TO OUR UNDULY HIGH   PUBLIC   SERVICE   RATES   IS ENFORCEMENT OF REASONABLE RATE-OF-RETURN CEILING TO BEGIN WITH, THE BASIC PREMISE OF DEMOCRATIC GOVERNANCE:

THE GREATEST GOOD FOR THE GREATEST NUMBER

Under Article II of the Constitution:"The Philippines is a democratic and republican state. Sovereignty resides in the people and all government authority emanates from them…. The prime duty of government is to serve and protect the people." In effect, our Constitution and laws have adopted the majority rule as normal basis of decision making, with simple majority of one or two-thirds majority as winning vote on crucial issues. In essence, MAJORITY RULE translates to THE GREATEST GOOD FOR THE GREATEST NUMBER under democratic governance. Free-market Economists have Ignored the Greatest Good for the Greatest Number in the Privatization of—or Awarding of Franchises in—Captive Markets Clothed with Public Interest, Thereby Resulting in Unduly High Public Service Rates. Our very high public service rates, which stick out like a sore thumb in Asia, is an economic problem that has victimized not only big and small businesses but also generally poor consumers and commuters nationwide. We have abnormally high power, water, telecom, and toll-road rates in the region. We also have very high medicine and agro-chemical prices. Forexample, our second highest power rates in Asia (next only to those in Japan) have for so long served as heavy burden to business and stumbling block to our rapid industrialization and faster economic growth.

THE ROOT AND COMMON DENOMINATOR OF OUR VERY HIGH PUBLIC SERVICE RATES: LACK OF ENFORCED RATE-

OF-RETURN CEILING ON ALL—REPEAT ALL— PUBLIC SERVICE PROVIDERS! HOW THIS CAME ABOUT IS UNFLATTERING TO THE PHILIPPINE ECONOMICS "PROFESSION"

There is a common denominator or cause of our unwarrantedly high public service rates in the power, water, telecom, toll-road, and probably other public service industries that cater to mass consumers and commuters—lackof properly enforced rate-of-return limit on government authorized public service providers. Obviously,if there is an effectively implemented profit-rate ceiling, EVEN IF THERE IS NO COMPETITION, public service rates cannot go beyond reasonable levels—this is basic and plain common sense.

Conversely, even if there are competing oligopolistic public service providers, if there is no prescribed profit-rate limit, cartelized operation or regulatory capture can easily nullify the price-lowering effect of competition. Root of Lack of Enforced Rate-of-Return Limit:Products of Local and Foreign Top Universities—Dominant Free-Market Economists Unskilled in the Fine Points of Properly Managing the Two Types of Market:

(1) the Really Free Market for Thousands of Ordinary Goods and Services, and

(2) the Captive Markets for Relatively Few Basic Necessities Clothed with Public Interest, to Which the Power, Water, Telecom, and Toll-Road Markets Belong.

From management audit standpoint, the Philippine economics "profession" has failed to help the government shape national economic policies and practices that spur economic development, promote equality and inclusive growth, maintain a fair balance between the conflicting interests of business and consumers, and bridge the gap between the poor and the rich. Our abnormally high power rates, for example, have long served as obstacle to our industrialization and fast economic growth, yet our economists in and out of government have not offered the readily available solution that will definitely bring down our country's second highest power rates in the region to reasonable level—strict enforcement of the Supreme-Court-ruled 12% rate-of-return limit, to be calculated based on net income beforeincome tax (ERB vs. Meralco, G.R. No. 141314, November 15, 2002).

As explained further later, Meralco's return on equity (ROE) as of 2015 stood at 31% before income tax and 24% after income tax, in violation of the Supreme Courtruling either way we look at it. Under the situation, if Meralco's rate of return is adjusted downward to 12% as required by jurisprudence, its rates will definitely go down, so why is the Philippine economics "profession" deafeningly silent on it, despite my repeated emails to key members of it in the past?

Thus, our high public service rates are caused by lack of properly enforced rate-of-return ceiling, rooted in turn from the failure of the academe in the Philippines and abroad to produce Filipino economists who can distinguish between— and treat differently—the two types of market: the really free market for ordinary goods and services and captive market for basic necessities clothed with public interest. We need economists who will enlighten the government toward the institution of sound economic policies and laws that promote the greatest good for the greatest number. What Competition as Price-Lowering Economic Tool Has Failed to Do Indirectly in Deregulated WESM under Fallacious EPIRA (RA9136)—Bring Down High Power Rates—Regulation with Proper Enforcement of Rate-of-Return Limit Will Do Directly in the Power Generation Industry, and Such Regulation Applies to Other Crucial Captive Markets as Well.

"Economists firmly believe that voluntary transactions in free markets tend to work toward the common good. But they also believe that nearly every participant in the market place would love to rig the system in his or her own favor." [Sean Masaki Flynn, Economics for Dummies (NJ:Wiley Publishing, Inc., 2005) p. 334]

Therefore, instituting free-market COMPETITION under DEREGULATION does not always mean low prices, because profit-maximizing market players will instinctively work for more profits for as Long as they can, as in the case especially of our ultra high medicine prices before the passage of the Cheaper Medicine Act in2008 (RA 9502).

As part of human nature and rapacious greed, despite presence of numerous suppliers, free market can yield high prices to the extent the MARKET CAN BEAR—without regard to actual low cost of goods sold by the competing market players, an advantage that they keep to themselves and do not share as price reduction to consumers—for as long as there is opportunity for "every participant in the market place... to rig the system in his or her own favor."

The government should be proactive, not reactive. It should plug vulnerabilities to, or opportunity for, market rigging. It should promptly institute the safety net against already existing—not just impending—unreasonable rates in the power, water, telecom, and probably other crucial captive markets: reasonable cap in rate of return.

Why Regulation of Captive Markets Will Not be Unfair to Public Service Providers: They Will Not be Forced Against their Will to Serve. They Will Serve the Captive Markets, With Sure Demand From Mass Consumers, Under Regulation Rules Set by the Government Because it is Still More Profitable for them to Do So Compared to Available Alternatives. In affirming its landmark decision that disallowed deduction from net income of corporate income tax in the reckoning of Meralco's entitlement to 12% reasonable return (ERB vs. Meralco,G.R. No. 141314, November 15, 2002), upon Meralco's appeal, the Supreme Courtruled further, as follows: "The business and operations of a public utility are imbued with public interest. In a very real sense, a public utility is engaged in public service—providing basic commodities and services indispensable to the interest of the general public. For this reason, a public utility submits to the regulation of government authorities and surrenders certain business prerogatives, including the amount of rates that may be charged by it." (Republic of the Philippines, represented by Energy Regulatory Board vs. Manila Electric Company, G.R. No. 141314, April, 9, 2003).

Pursuant to this Supreme Court declaration, in the privatization of government public-utility operations and awarding of franchises to public service companies, like those in the power, water, telecom, and toll-road industries, the government should set franchise or concession conditions protective of consumers and commuters—such as 12% or lower rate-of-return ceiling. For as long as there are takers—which means that the government franchise or concession conditions are still more advantageous to private investors compared to their opportunity cost, the government should stick to those conditions. Only if there are no takers should the government sweeten the pot to attract investors.

WHY THE ACADEME CAN STAND IMPROVEMENT ON WHAT IT IS TEACHING AND NOT TEACHING

In systems work, the diametrically opposed economic conditions of really free market and captive market imbued with public interest definitely need separate and distinctly different treatments, but notice that our dominant economists in government and academe—seemingly illiterate in the fine points of control and systems "discipline"—have espoused the same free-market approach to both kinds of markets. As they are products of educational institutions, it seems the academecan stand improvement in what it is teaching and not teaching. With due respect to our economists produced by UP, Ateneo, La Salle, UA&P, Harvard, etc. it appears that they have failed to demonstrate their expertise on what business to regulate and not to regulate,and how to properly regulate those that need regulation, like monopolies affected with public interest, which have to be either prohibited or regulated pursuant to Section 19, Article XII of the Constitution. They seem unskilled in systems work and lacking in problem-solving expertise.

- The first and foremost example of lack of problem-solving skill among economists was their inability to come up with less disastrous solutions to dollar speculation, which provoked peso depreciation, exchange losses, and inflation during the Asian meltdown.

To illustrate, in the 1997-1998 Asian crisis, IMF-prescribed and central-bank implemented back-breaking high interest rates of as much as roughly 40%, which wrought havoc in the Philippine banking system and borrowing sector, culminating in unprecedented P600 BILLION bad loans (Mario B. Casayuran, "Senate Oks asset, dual citizenship bills," Manila Bulletin, October 24, 2002, page1), equated to 36% of total bank lending. The destabilizing and bankruptcy inducing bad loans necessitated the subsequent passage of the Special Purpose Vehicle Act (RA 9182) to address this problem, which plagued our economy for many years. ANNEX A—with excerpts from mybook Puzzlers: Economic Sting, published in 2005— shows why IMF's high-interest-rate economic solution, the scourge of economies in the Asian meltdown, was unsound economics and wrong: it had monumental fallacies and less disastrous alternatives and could have been avoided but was not.

How it came to pass is astounding because solving it was the subject of Bangko Sentral committee hearings conducted by eminent Monetary Board members, one of whom became Secretary of Economic Planning while another was an economics professor, with PhD from a top US university appended to his name. As reported by Bangko Sentral, its committee hearings were attended by representatives from Ateneo Dept. of Economics, UP School of Economics, UP Cebu, Southwestern University, University of San Juan Recoletos, University of the Visayas, and St. Theresas's College,

    - The second case in point: economists failed to see that return on rate base (RORB), with rate base defined as assets in operation, mandated under Section 12 of the MWSS Charter (RA 6234), is a WRONG and useless profit-rate limit, because it is an ultra high rate-of-return ceiling that cannot be breached except when the rate of return is extremely high.

    The reckoning of allowable rate of return as enshrined in one of our laws, the MWSS Charter (RA 6234), is return on rate base (RORB), with rate base defined as assets in operation (plus two months working capital). This provision in Section 12 of the MWSS Charter has been fallaciously adopted underSection 9.1, Article 9 of the MWSS concession contracts with Maynilad and Manila Water. As illustrated in ANNEX B, RORB is illogical and entails DOUBLE RECKONING of RETURN on assets inoperation financed by CREDITORS:

    - First, as interest expense payable to creditors on their loans used to acquire the assets; and,

    - Second, as 12% allowable return to stockholders on total assets in operation—erroneously including the assets financed by creditors, probably on the wrong and insufficient ground that it is part of total company assets. Corresponding return has already been reckoned on the creditor-financed assets by way of the cited interest expense payable to creditors, hence it is WRONG to reckon for the SECOND TIME a return on these assets in favor of stockholders who did not finance their acquisition.

THE FUNDAMENTAL SOLUTION TO OUR UNDULY HIGH PUBLIC SERVICE RATES THAT HAS ELUDED FOR SO LONG OUR HIGHLY EDUCATED ECONOMISTS AND FINANCE EXPERTS IN AND OUT OF GOVERNMENT AND ACADEME: PROPER ENFORCEMENT OF RATE-OF-RETURN CEILING TO PUBLIC SERVICEPROVIDERS—THE SAFETY NET AGAINSTOVERPRICING

There is a basic and common-sense solution that has been lacking and has seemingly eluded even our reputable economic and finance experts—proper enforcement of reasonable rate-of-return ceiling, which currently stands at 12% for public utility monopolies, as ruled by the Supreme Court in 1966 and reiterated in 2002 (ERB vs. Meralco, G.R. No. 141314, November 15, 2002). The lack of proper enforcement of needed rate-of-return ceiling stems from the following:

1.	Lack of proper regulation of oligopolies in captive markets affected with public interest, such as those in the telecom industry, followed by those in the power generation industry which have been deregulated under the Electric Power Industry ReformAct (EPIRA) of 2001 (RA 9136).	2. Lack of proper regulation of even the monopolies already subject to regulation pursuant to Section 19, Article XII of the Constitution—those operating in captive markets for public services clothed with public interest, such as in the power, water, and toll-road industries. Following are the key performance indicators of lack of proper regulation of monopolies Meralco and Maynilad Water: their excessively high rates of return on equity (ROE) based on their annual financial reports to stockholders and Securities and Exchange Commission (SEC): Meralco ROE:

2011: 20%
2012: 25%
2013: 23%
2014: 23%
2015: 24%

The foregoing rates of ROE were calculated based on the conventional method of reckoning profit: net income AFTER income tax. If the rate of return is determined based on the Supreme Court ruling that disallowed INCOME TAX deduction in the reckoning of reasonable rate of return for public utilities, Meralco's ROE based on net income BEFORE income tax is a whopping 31% in 2015!

Maynilad ROE:

2008: 247%
2009: 147%
2010: 82%
2011: 59%
2012: 44%

The above ultra high rates of ROE obviously equated to unreasonably high service rates to consumers and violated their Supreme-Court ruled right to be charged reasonable rates (ERB vs. Meralco, G.R. No. 141314,November 15, 2002).

HOW TO ENFORCERATE-OF-RETURN LIMIT UNDER PROPER REGULATION OF MONOPOLIES AND OLIGOPOLIES IN CAPTIVE

MARKETS   FOR   BASIC   NECESSITIES
AFFECTED WITH PUBLIC INTEREST

Under a system of fair and justifiable regulation, reasonable rate-of-return limit can—and should—be applied to all monopolistic and oligopolistic public service providers in captive markets clothed with public interest, including the power-generator oligopoly deregulated under EPIRA (RA 9136).

Why power generators should be subjected to12% or lower rate-of-return limit, with concomitant amendment of EPIRA, is explained in ANNEX C.

How to institute proper regulation is presented in a chapter of my book manuscript in progress, which deals with captive market economics vs. privatization.

In closing, let me state that all reforms aimed at public-service-rate reduction have to culminate in the same safety net against overpriced public service rates—reasonable rate-of-return ceiling to public service providers that equates to reasonable rates to the paying public. If there is a "magic formula" toward reasonable power, water, telecom, toll-road, and other service rates in captive markets imbued with public interest, this is it. There seems no alternative to it. Can members of the Philippine economics "profession" find a substitute to it? If they can, let them come up with it—in service of the people, the government, and their own families.

Sincerely,

MARCELO L. TECSON

A CPA and Concerned Citizen Former Controller, Petron Corporation; Former Head of

Planning Group, PNOC Energy Companies; Former Head of Planning Group and Internal Audit & Systems in the then local subsidiary of a US multinational oil company; Former Chief Accountant and later Financial and Management Service Chief of what is now the Departmentof Energy (DOE), where he gained insights on how to fight corruption in government

Email: martecson@yahoo.com
San Miguel,Bulacan
9- 7-16, 9-16-16

Cc through separate letters/emails: Select executive and legislative government officials
Select members of media, academe, andeconomic society   Select civil society groups and concerned citizens, etc.

=====

ANNEX A EXPOSED AT LAST IN THIS BOOK! HIGH INTEREST RATES IN THE ASIAN CRISIS, ORCHESTRATED BY IMF AND CENTRAL BANKS DESPITE BUILT-IN SUBSIDY AND AVAILABLE LESS DISASTROUS ALTERNATIVES THEREFORE, CONSEQUENT HIGH BAD LOANS ARE DUE TO THEIR FAULT! THE ECONOMIC STING CONDONED BY THE GOVERNMENT, ACADEME, AND ECONOMISTS: VERY HIGH INTEREST RATES—ONLY IN THE PHILIPPINES PRIME LENDING RATES   BANK SPREADS

	Asiaweek issues:	10-24-97	11-14-97	
2-06-98				3-27-98
February1998				
Korea	8.50			8.50
11.50	11.50		0.8	
Malaysia	9.55	10.10	10.45	

12.00   1.0   Thailand 13.75   13.75
14.75   14.75   3.9
 Philippines 32.00 36.00   25.05   24.00
10.4 ·

Above statistics (in percent per annum) which originated from Bangko Sentral ng Pilipinas (BSP) and media, suggest that only BSP seriously took and naively followed to superfluous extent IMF's 60%high-interest- rate prescription in the Asian crisis—even if it could have resisted because, at that time, the Philippines had mere contagion crisis, it had strong economic fundamentals, it did not beg for multi-billion- dollar IMFbailout fund asked by other crisis-hit Asian nations, BSP had less punishing high-interest- rate alternatives sleeping right in its own old circulars, and countries hit harder by crisis managed to maintain interest rates at much lower levels. BSP kowtowed to IMF—to the benefit of BANKS.

At very high interest rates, local bank spreads eventually breached 20%, while countless true owners of lent-out funds—depositors—were not compensated for inflation loss. They continued to receive the same interest income of as low as 2% on their savings accounts—despite doubled bank lending rates—and suffered negative real interest rates from double-digit inflation rate. BSP made the real-interest- rate wisdom a sham in the Asian crisis—at the expense of DEPOSITORS.

Free-market apostles IMF and BSP abhor subsidies that distort market prices, vitiate free market, and encourage wasteful consumption by subsidized sectors. Incredibly, in the Asian flu, they operated their own disastrous subsidy scheme. Locally, they forced three million sacrificed borrowers, no matter how poor, to bear BSP's tight-money policy implementation cost—in the form of high interest rates, exacted from discriminated borrowers beyond the limits of sanity: in excess of their capacity to pay and up to the point of loan defaults or even bankruptcies, while more than 70 million free-lunching non-borrowers, no matter how rich, equally "benefited" from BSP's policy measure but did not share in its cost, a classic case of unsound economics that culminated in PhP600 billion or 36% bad loans in the banking system—at the expense of BORROWERS.

HOW THE PHILIPPINE ECONOMICS "PROFESSION" FAILED TO TAME FALLACIOUS HIGH INTEREST RATES IN THE ASIAN CRISIS THAT WROUGHT HAVOC IN THE ECONOMY BY WAY OF BAD LOANS TO BANKS AND BANKRUPTCIES TO BORROWERS
     - Objectives of high interest rates in the Asian crisis:
 The conventional high-interest- rate economic wisdom is normally employed by monetary authorities to attain the chain objectives of minimized borrowing, tightened money supply, discouraged currency speculation, stabilized exchange rate, curbed currency depreciation, and ultimately contained inflation. [Marcelo L. Tecson, Sr., Puzzlers: Economic Sting (MakatiCity, Philippines: Raiders of the Lost Gold Publication, 2005), pp. 1, 16-18,104]. From the then IMF Managing Director Michel Camdessus himself:
 "To reverse (currency depreciation) , countries have to make it more attractive to hold domestic

currency, and that means temporarily raising interest rates, even if this (hurts) weak banks and corporations. "(" Doctor Knows Best?" Asiaweek, July 17, 1998, p. 46): Fromformer BSP Governor Gabriel Singson: Bangko Sentral ng Pilipinas (BSP) had to raise interest rates to 30%"middle ground" rate to discourage currency speculators during the Asiancrisis. ("Bangko Sentral chief: Worst is over," MarketWatch, June 1999, p. 9).

- The high-interest- rate solution to dollar speculation was unnecessary because there were available less disastrous high-interest- rate alternatives, but IMF and central banks appeared clueless about them.

As expounded on in my book published in 2005—Puzzlers: Economic Sting—following were the available less punishing alternatives to high interest rates, languishing in BSP's own old circulars, unrecognized by the then crop of central bankers and unimplemented by BSP economists even when needed most during the Asian turbulence:

a. Control vs. premature dollar demand by non-speculators: forward cover. For a fee, those with foreign obligations but not yet due can be discouraged from prematurely paying their dollar loans (which raises dollar demand) through BSP's currency risk protection program. (References: BSPCircular No. 149 dated December 22, 1997; BSP Circular No. 174 dated September 2, 1998: BSP Circular No. 261 dated October 12, 2000.)

b. Control vs. non-bank dollar speculators: documentation requirement (or proof of foreign obligations) for dollar purchases by end-users. Dollar purchases that cannot be substantiated by the required proof, like import invoices, are obviously for speculation or hoarding, therefore these should not be allowed. Without this more basic measure, banks can wantonly sell dollars to speculators, in the process bring down their dollar holdings below their limits, after which they can again buy replenishment dollars. (References: BSP Circular 138 datedJuly 31, 1997, which is an amendment of central bank regulations originally issued when the old Central Bank of the Philippines shifted to decontrol in1962); BSP Circular 162 dated April 7, 1998; BSP Circular 264 dated October 27,2000)

c. Control vs. bank speculators: cap in bank dollar holdings. With this regulation, even if banks will speculate in dollars, they can do soup to their dollar holding limits only. (References: BSP Circular No. 137 dated July 31, 1997; BSPCircular Letter dated October 24, 1997; BSP Circular No. 171 dated August 29,1998)

Why Couldn't Local and International Experts Fathom, or Think of on Their Own, What Pioneering Visionary Filipino Central Bankers Conjured Ages Ago And Left Enshrined in Today's Long Standing Philippine Central Bank Circulars—Currency Speculation Control? "Still no solution, central bankers share gripes on speculation" The Bank for International Settlements, a "Swiss-based organization, which acts as a clearing house for the world's central banks, organized the meeting of...monetary chiefs at its HongKong office. US Federal Reserve chair Alan Greenspan attended the meeting as part of his tour through Asia." Result of the meeting: "Central bankers from around the globe have found no immediate solution to a question that has troubled Asian leaders for nearly two years: How to control speculators...."   —AP, Philippine Daily Inquirer,January 13, 1999, p. B5 What BSP failed to recognize—which it even amended—its own regulation vs. dollar speculation! On sales of foreign exchange by authorized agent banks (AABs), "AABs may sell foreign exchange to residents...for any non-trade purpose, without the need of Bangko Sentral...approval, provided that:

a) for sales...exceeding $25,000,the AAB shall require...supporting documents (proof of foreign obligations) from the purchaser of the foreign exchange...."   —BSP Circular No. 138, Series of 1997, dated July 31, 1997 Just where was BSP's problem in stopping currency speculation? Those buying dollars for the payment of foreign obligations are legitimate end-users, not speculators. Those purchasing dollars but not for the payment of foreign obligations because they have none are—-what else if not hoarders or speculators? They may include legitimate savers in dollars but during times of crisis when dollar demand hasto be managed, they are saver-hoarders just the same. If speculators are without foreign obligations, then they do not have proof of such obligations. Once they attempt to buy dollars and are asked by forex traders to submit the required proof pursuant to BSP Circular No. 138, they cannot comply, hence they cannot buy dollars. Thus, provided properly implemented, this BSP circular would prevent would-be speculators from buying and speculating in dollars. So, where was BSP's problem in stopping dollar speculation that, as admitted by BSP Governor Gabriel Singson himself, it had to raise interest rates to 30% "middle ground" rate just to discourage currency speculators during the Asian crisis? ("Bangko Sentral chief: Worst is over," MarketWatch, June 1999, p. 9).

- At last, in August 2001, the Philippine central bank successfully enforced CURRENCY SPECULATION CONTROL through running after erring banks that had been in violation of BSP Circular 138. BSP had repeatedly received the suggestion to run after and punish economic-saboteur dollar speculators—in other words, implement currency speculation control—such as that presented in my letters and papers dated as follows: April 1, July 20, August 22, and October 22 in 1998; January 12, May 16, and June 24 in 1999; June 12, October 2, October 29, and December 18 in 2000; and January 23, February 18, March 22, June 30, and August 4 in 2001.

When, due to confluence of events that would have pictured Bangko Sentral ng Pilipinas as coddler of dollar speculators—including dollar-speculating banks—if it would still not run after them through strictly enforcing BSP Circular 138, BSP did in August 2001 what it had evaded doing since 1997—acting directly against dollar-speculating banks by penalizing them, as well as exposing their names to media and subjecting them to the risk of public backlash—the PESO SUDDENLY RECOVERED from P53.05 to P51.85 to the dollar even without high interest rates! "A trader pointed out that where sophisticated measures like the forward cover called Currency Risk Protection Program and other similar moves have failed...all the central bank had to do was shame the bankers' lot and voila, the peso rose by P1.15...from P53.... It took only a two-page press statement, detailing each bank's violation and fine...for the local currency to achieve some semblance of peace and quiet after two months of unrest" that SANK THE PESO TO THE DEPTH of P54.335 the previous month. (Clarissa S.Batino, "BSP cracks whip on 'old boys' club," Philippine Daily Inquirer, August 13, 2001, p. C1). If shaming dollar-speculating or dollar-speculation- abetting banks worked wonders, how much more if BSP would expel and prosecute erring bank officials? The recovery of the local currency was attained, sustained, and even improved further to less than P50 to the dollar as of first half 2002, while interest rates stabilized at one of the lowest levels in years.

============

ANNEX BX
ILLUSTRATIVE EXAMPLE OF MONUMENTAL ERROR IN USING RETURN ON RATE BASE (RORB) AS RATE-OF-RETURN CEILINGFOR PUBLIC SERVICE COMPANIES THAT USE BORROWEDFUNDS

Let us assume the following financial data (in Philippine pesos): Assets in operation(99 funded by loans and 1 by equity) .... 100Liabilities (Loans)..... .... 99 Equity(Capital) ....1 Interest on loans (loan balances constant during the year) ..... 11.88Net income for the year...... 12 The respective returns tocreditors and stockholders are as follows: Rate of return to creditors: Interest payments to creditors, 11.88 over99 loans .... 12% Rates of return to stockholders: RORB: 12 net income over 99 + 1 or 100 assets in operation ..... 12% ROE: 12 net income over 1 Equity 1,200%

Analysis of Financial Statistics

a. Return to Creditors: The creditors' return on loans used toacquire P99 worth of assets consists of the P11.88 or 12% interest on loansincurred by the company as interest expense, thereby resulting in reduced netincome already net of creditors' return on the assets financed by them.

b. Return to Stockholders: For their 12% maximum RORB, with assets used in operation as rate base, corporate stockholders are entitled to P12 net income or 12% return on P100 total assets used in operation. The P12 net income is broken down as follows:

(1) P11.88 or12% return on the P99 assets financed by creditors, and

(2) P0.12 or 12% returnon the P1 asset acquired out of stockholders' capital investment or equity.

Clearly, under fallacious RORB, there is double reckoning of return on the P99 creditor-financed assets—first, to creditors as P11.88 interest on loans, and second, to stockholders as P11.88 net income even if they were not the ones who funded the acquisition of the P99 assets. The result is pure and simple DOUBLE BILLING to consumers. In the example, the stockholders wil lrecover within one year 12 times their invested capital or equity, yet they will still NOT EXCEED the prescribed 12% RORB ceiling, exactly the reason why, in the case of Maynilad, despite its unconscionably high rates of return on equity (ROE) of as much as 247% in 2008 and 147% in 2009 based on its annual reports to stockholders, it did not exceed the 12% RORB ceiling imposed by Section 12 of RA 6234 (MWSS Charter) as well as by Article 9, Section 9.1 of the MWSS concession agreement that adopted the 12% RORB limit set by the MWSS Charter.

============   =========

ANNEX C

AS CHANGE FOR THE BETTER UNDER PRIVATIZATION—FROM GOVERNMENT MONOPOLY WITHOUT COMPETITION TO PRIVATE OLIGOPOLY WITH PRICE-LOWERING COMPETITION—PRIVATE POWER GENERATORS SHOULD BESUBJECT TO 12% OR LOWER RATE-OF-RETURN CEILING, OTHERWISE IT IS NOT A CHANGE FOR THEBETTER

If regulated monopolies like public utilities are entitled to 12% maximum return on investment (ROI) under a 1966 Supreme Court ruling on Meralco, reiterated in its landmark decision on Meralco corporate income tax (ERB vs, Meralco, G.R.NO. 141314, November 15, 2002), then as change for the better under EPIRA-mandated privatization, competing deregulated private generators should be entitled to less than 12% ROI, or at most equal to it, otherwise the change will be from bad to worse. Privatization in the power generation industry is a shift from regulated government monopoly without competition—the power-generator National Power Corporation (NAPOCOR)—to deregulated private oligopoly with supposed competition. It is supposed to be a change for the better, from a monopoly without competitors to oligopoly with price-lowering competition.

If so, as key performance indicator (KPI) of the change for the better, as regulated monopolies NAPOCOR and Meralco, as well as other public utility monopolies, are entitled to maximum 12% return on investment as ruled by the Supreme Court (ERBvs. Meralco, G.R. No. 141314, November 15, 2002), then—as proof of change for the better—the private oligopoly with competition should be entitled to return on investment lower than, or at most equal to, the12% rate-of-return ceiling for the cited monopolies without competition—otherwise what is privatization with competition for? Unfortunately, this safety net against overpricing has not been injected into the government's management of the power industry—resulting in the rise, rather than reduction, of our power rates that have earned the notorious distinction of being highest in the region except Japan. It will not be surprising if this way of ensuring change for the better may have never even occurred to our government planning, economic, and financial experts who, if asked, may not know even if deregulated oligopolistic power generation companies are already exploiting unfettered free market—through overpricing as may be betrayed by excessively high actual rates of return on their investments. This utter lack of consumer protection against overpricing under fallacious privatization is an example of why we cannot leave everything to economists.

Sincerely,
MARCELO L. TECSON
September 16, 2016

ooO0Ooo

4.

Saving Duterte

Narciso Reyes Jr.

Dateline, Philippine Daily Inquirer
September 20, 2016
Excerpts

"THE STRONG do as they will...The weak suffer as they must."

The Greek historian Thucydides made that memorable observation to describe the behavior of states as they struggled for power and survival in the Aegean region in 416 B.C. One could easily connect this dictum to President Duterte's perspective on how to rule and transform the Philippines: by using a mailed-fist "might is right" approach to law and order" a merciless view that is governed by no scruples except the morality of realpolitik and desired results.

No one can doubt Mr. Duterte's guts. "He has tons of it," as one admirer, F. Sionil Jose, put it. He is not afraid to challenge anyone and any institution that gets in his way: the Catholic Church, its leader, Pope Francis, the United Nations, our Supreme Court, Congress, and the international and local media. Not even the world's superpower,the United States, is exempt from his wrath. Obviously, he does not believe in the wisdom of "speaking softly while carrying a bigstick," to paraphrase Theodore Roosevelt, an American president renowned for his physical courage and Machiavellian statecraft.

But one wishes that our primary leader could learn how to hold his intemperate tongue and select only key battles in order to save his precious time and resources, as well as his political capital that is being dissipated and squandered on various battlegrounds.

His unwillingness to modify his perspectives, strategy and tactics could be his worst enemy. And the country will needlessly suffer the consequences. Saving Mr. Duterte, from himself, should thus assume top priority among his advisers and supporters. In the words of Vice President Leni Robredo, "he is the only president we have, and it's our obligation to support him … even while disagreeing with some of his actions… The country cannot afford another upheaval."

There are two major divisive issues that could derail the Duterte locomotive from its goal of an inclusively "prosperous, peaceful Philippines:" his decision to bury the dictator Ferdinand Marcos' remains in the Libingan ng mga Bayani and his velvet-glove approach to China at the expense of the Philippines' longtime ally, America.

Mr. Duterte's stubborn decision to proceed with the Marcos burial, despite its highly questionable basis, will continue to be a highly contentious issue. It will not die with the burial in the Libingan because thousands of lives "among the country's best and brightest" were lost or ruined during the dictatorship, as the economy was systematically plundered by the Marcoses and their cronies. Thus, the Marcos legacy cannot be allowed to be revised and airbrushed through the Libingan. If the burial goes through, Mr. Duterte will have provided his enemies and critics with a generous unsolicited gift that will serve to remind people of a dark chapter in our history, and his strange misreading of it.

The political capital he could lose will not be something to sneeze at. Paradoxically, Marcos' burial in the Libingan is totally unnecessary because it is well-known that he wished to be buried in Batac, beside his beloved mother's grave.

Foreign affairs is the other face of a country's domestic policy. When world leaders go to the negotiating table, they carry with them the hopes, anxieties, fears and aspirations of their peoples.

Our President is a proud and volatile man, and his first foray into international diplomacy at the recent Asean Summit in Laos reveals that side in him. He knows our colonial history and how America waged its "first Vietnam" in the Philippines, resulting in many Filipino (including Moro) deaths. So it's understandable that he would brook nomoralistic lecturing from US President Barack Obama, even if the latter represents the most powerful nation on earth.

But as the leader representing the interests of over 100 million Filipinos, Mr. Duterte must learn how to manage his temper tantrums "so unpresidential" on the global stage.

After all, the world has dramatically changed since 1901. America has mellowed and become a reluctant, world-weary global policeman. China, on the other hand, has transformed into a rising, power-hungry regional hegemon that wants to gobble up almost the entire South China Sea; does not give a hoot about the recent ruling of the Permanent Court of Arbitration calling China's claim to the disputed waters illegal; and, in a "reverse opium war," continues to coddle syndicates that smuggle dangerous drugs into the Philippines" a hostile act Malacañang itself acknowledged.

Economically, the Philippines gains much more from America than it does from China, according to the World Bank. Filipinos are also more comfortable with American values and aspirations; that's why more than three million of us live in the United States. Furthermore, China's economic future is under a dark cloud while America's is much brighter.

Big nations still flex their muscle and the weaker must suffer. But in our tightly-wired, interdependent world, there is really no such thing as an "independent foreign policy." Today's nations all live in varying degrees of entangled relations with one another. Even the hermit kingdom of North Korea depends on its chief patron, China, to survive.

Let's not fight a longtime ally and weaken our negotiating hand. China plays clever geopolitical poker. The Philippines should, too.

Narciso   Reyes
Jr.(ngreyes1640@hotmail.com) is an international
book author and former diplomat. He lived in
Beijing in 1978-81 as bureau chief of the Philippine
News Agency.

source: winda at moonglowplanet

ooOOoo

5.

The Victims of the Davao Death Squad: Consolidated Report 1998-2015

Fr. Amado Picardal, CSsR

(About the Author: Fr. Picarel is a Catholic Priest,
Executive Secretary od CBCP-BEC Committee, Serving
Redemptorist Congregation, Licentiate in Theology
(Jesuit School of Theology at Berkeley, California),
Doctorate in Theology (Gregorian University, Rome), Pro-
life & Peace Activist around the Philippines. Barefoot
Pilgrim of Camino de Santiago. Ran/walked across the
Philippines. Interests include Scuba-diving,
mountaineering, Poetry, Music (piano, violin, guitar, flute,
song-writing), Holistic, Healing, Christian-Muslim
dialogue, Basic Ecclesial Communities.)

Dateline, Tuesday, April 19, 2016

I recently received a consolidated report of the killings perpetrated by the Davao Death Squad (DDS) since 1998 up to the end of 2015. The source will not be mentioned for obvious reasons. Suffice it to say that since the killings started, they have been monitoring these cases. I know them very well and I have been collaborating with them as we denounced these killings and worked with the Commission of Human Rights and the Human Rights Watch. They are hesitant to make the report public out of apprehension that it will be used for political purposes. I believe that to hide this would be a disservice to the nation since I believe that the body count could multiply many times over throughout the whole country in the next six years. The original report that I have is in Excel format, and very detailed (year by year, according to age, sex, areas, weapons used, etc). What I present is a summary and my own analysis. I know that when I do this, I am risking my life. But the truth must come out before it is too late.

The total number of persons killed by the DDS from 1998-2015 is 1,424. Let me repeat in words – ONE THOUSAND FOUR HUNDRED TWENTY-FOUR victims. This can be considered as MASS MURDER perpetrated by the same group, inspired and supported by the same persons. The data does not include those killed in other cities where the DDS have expanded franchise-style.

Out of 1,424, there were 1,367 male and 57 female. This means that those murdered by the

DDS were not only men, there were also fifty-seven women.

Looking at this according to age there were 132 children killed (17 and below) — 126 boys and 6 girls. The youngest was a 12 years boy and a 15 year girl. There was a 9 year old boy who was killed by a stray bullet – he was not an intended target.

There was a total of 476 young adults (18-25) murdered – 466 male, 19 female. The number of older adults (26 years and above) killed were 612 (466 male, 28 female). There were victims whose age were not given – 201 (191 male, 10 female).

Thus, almost 50 percent of the victims were young people (children and young adults). Most the victims were killed in urban poor areas (e.g. Buhangin, Agdao, Bangkerohan, Boulevard, Matina, Toril). Most of those killed were involved in illegal drugs – as users and pushers. There were also those involved in petty crimes – theft, cellphone snatching, gang members. There were 14 cases of mistaken identity – they were not the intended targets but the DDS hit men mistakenly hit the wrong target. There were some who had gone away after being warned that they were on the hit list and after some years, after reforming their lives, came back thinking that they were safe. Their names were still on the list so they were still killed.

Thus, one can say that majority of the victims of the DDS were young and poor – juvenile delinquents considered as the weeds of society. There were no reports of drug lords or big time criminals among those killed by the DDS. There were two journalists who were believed to have been murdered by the DDS – Jun Pala and Ferdie "Batman" Limtungan. Jun Pala was a radio commentator who constantly spoke out against the DDS and Mayor Duterte. There were two previous attempts on his life and he accused Duterte of being behind these attacks. He was finally killed by motorcycle riding men on the third try. Ferdie "Batman" Lintuan also spoke out against the DDS and also the alleged anomalies in the construction of the People's Park which he linked with Mayor Duterte. He was also killed by motorcycle riding men.

The victims of the DDS were unarmed. They did not fight back. Many were just sitting down on street-corners outside sari-sari stores, talking with friends and then suddenly shot in cold blood. There were some who were just released from prison and while waiting for public transportation on the side of the road were suddenly shot by motorcycling men. How the DDS knew the exact time and place they were to be released is amazing. Another victim was killed inside his home in front of his mother and three children who were begging the DDS not to kill him. One of the most well-known case is Clarita Alia – a vegetable vendor in Bangkerohan – whose teen-age sons (who were below 17 years old) were murdered by the DDS. I was asked by Clarita to bless the body of her boy, Fernando before he was buried.

I have personally witnessed the aftermath of two DDS killings. The first was in our parish church in Bajada. While officiating a Wedding Mass I heard shots outside in the carpark. I immediately rushed outside after the Mass to find out what happened. I saw the body of a teen-age boy lying in our church ground surrounded by people. He had just been shot by DDS hit-men while sitting in the car park with his friends. The killers escaped on a motor-cycle. There was a police car nearby but the police just fired warning shots into the air and did not go after the killers. The boy who was killed lived in a nearby slums area. He had been suspected as one of those who broke the window of a car park in our church and stole some items two weeks earlier.

The second time I witnessed the aftermath of a DDS killing was while mountain-biking in Lomondao, a distant barangay in Davao. As I neared the place I met three motorcycle riding men speeding back to the city. When I arrived in the place I saw people who gathered around the body of a young boy. When I asked what happened, someone told me it was the DDS. The boy was cell-phone snatcher and drug user. He added, the boy deserved to die.

The killings have not stopped. The DDS continue their murderous spree even to this day. For the last five years (2011-2015), there were 385 victims of extrajudicial killings in Davao – 39 of them below seventeen years old and 118 young adults (18-25). In 2011 there 111 reported DDS killings, in 2012 there were 61, in 2013 there were 101, in 2014 there were 52 and there were 60 in 2015. The DDS usually take a break during the campaign period. They will continue their operations after the elections.

So far, no one has been held accountable for these killings. There has been no official investigation by the police or the city government. The police do not acknowledge the existence of the

DDS. The Commission on Human Rights (CHR) came to Davao for a public hearing and also met secretly with witnesses – family of the victims and former members of DDS. Although the CHR recommended prosecution, this could not prosper because nobody was willing to testify in court out of fear. The DDS are still around and anybody who testifies will surely be targeted for assassination. I have met some of these witnesses and understand their fear. They claimed that some of those listed as victims were their former companions who knew too much and were suspected of betraying the DDS. So while former DDS members talked about how they were recruited, trained and how they operate, and who their handlers were and their link with some police and local government officials, all these information could not stand in court because they were not willing to testify in spite of the sworn statements made before the CHR. Much of the information can also be found in the report of the Human Rights Watch in 2009 *You Can Die Anytime: Death Squad Killings in Mindanao.* One of the findings of the Human Rights Watch report reveals the link between the DDS and the police:

"According to these "insiders," most members of the DDS are either former communist New People's Army insurgents who surrendered to the government or young men who themselves were death squad targets and joined the group to avoid being killed. Most can make far more money with the DDS than in other available occupations. Their handlers, called amo (boss), are usually police officers or ex-police officers. They provide them with training, weapons and ammunition, motorcycles, and information on the targets. Death

squad members often use .45-caliber handguns, a weapon commonly used by the police but normally prohibitively expensive for gang members and common criminals.

The insiders told Human Rights Watch that the amo obtain information about targets from police or barangay (village or city district) officials, who compile lists of targets. The amo provides members of a death squad team with as little as the name of the target, and sometimes an address and a photograph. Police stations are then notified to ensure that police officers are slow to respond, enabling the death squad members to escape the crime scene, even when they commit killings near a police station."

The Human Rights Watch Report also revealed the modus operandi:

"Our research found that the killings follow a pattern. The assailants usually arrive in twos or threes on a motorcycle without a license plate. They wear baseball caps and buttoned shirts or jackets, apparently to conceal their weapons underneath. They shoot or, increasingly, stab their victim without warning, often in broad daylight and in presence of multiple eyewitnesses, for whom they show little regard. And as quickly as they arrive, they ride off—but almost always before the police appear."

"They deserved to die." This is what Mayor Duterte said while denying involvement in these extrajudicial killings. At one time, he read a list in his TV program. A few weeks later many of those in the list were killed by the DDS.

"They deserve to die." This is also the attitude of many residents of the city towards the

victims of the DDS. This shows who are behind them and why there has been little outcry regarding these mass murders.

It appears that the DDS killings are the center-piece of Mayor Duterte's campaign against criminality in Davao City. To fight against criminality, you simply kill the criminals through extra-judicial executions carried out by the DDS. No need to arrest them, put them on trial and imprison them if proven guilty. No need for due process of the law. Criminals do not have rights – that is a western concept. For criminals there can only be one punishment – death. It doesn't matter if you are a petty criminal – even if you are only a drug addict or pusher or cell-phone snatcher, you deserve to die. The killings are meant to be a deterrent to crime – to instill fear on everyone so that they will stop committing crime. According to Human Rights Watch Report:

"The continued death squad operation reflects an official mindset in which the ends are seen as justifying the means. The motive appears to be simple expedience: courts are viewed as slow or inept. The murder of criminal suspects is seen as easier and faster than proper law enforcement. Official tolerance and support of targeted killing of suspected criminals promotes rather than curbs the culture of violence that has long plagued Davao City and other places where such killings occur."

It has been very difficult to speak out against these extrajudicial killings because majority of the people in Davao support these. The archdiocese of Davao under the leadership of Archbishop Fernando Capalla came out with a pastoral letter: "Thou Shalt Not Kill" and held several prayer vigils. We were a minority – a small voice whose cry in the wilderness was drowned out by the applause of the majority. The blood of 1,424 victims of the DDS was the price that was paid so that there could be peace and order – so that all can walk at night without fear. This was the peace of the cemetery, an order maintained by death squads – by criminals.

And the mass murder continues and there will be more blood spilled – not just in Davao but the entire Philippines. Mayor Duterte promised that if elected "the 1,000 will become 100,000." He declared that "it will be bloody." He said there will be" no need for more jails — just funeral parlors." He promised to "eliminate criminality in the entire country within 3-6 months." How will he do it? The answer is what happened in Davao – through the DDS under the direction of many police officers who deny their existence, with the financial support coming from businessmen and also drawn from the government coffers.

"I'm willing to go to hell, as long as the people I serve live in paradise." Is this an admission on the part of Mayor Duterte that what he has done is a grave sin against God that could someday earn him divine punishment?

Is Davao a paradise after 18 years of DDS extrajudicial killings? Has criminality been eradicated? According to the data from PNP covering 2010-2015, out of 15 chartered cities Davao was fourth in terms of Total Index of Crimes: 37,797 incidents. In terms of murder, Davao was no. 1 (1,032 incidents) and in terms of rape Davao was no. 2 (843 incidents). This report gives the impression that in Davao you can be murdered and raped any time. Murder is not really that bad if the DDS and the Mayor can do it. Rape is not really that bad if the Mayor can callously joke about it, wishing he was the first in line when he heard that a hostage – an Australian Lay Missionary – was raped.

Meanwhile, the families of victims cry out for justice as the DDS continue their killing spree. The national government has failed to address this mass murder that could soon multiply many times over, God forbid.

If the DDS is not stopped and those behind it is not held accountable, there will be a national bloodbath. Those who support it and allow it to multiply will have blood in their hands – they will be accomplices to mass murder. The one who orders this is a mass murderer – the biggest Criminal of them all.

If it is alright to kill suspected criminals – who can stop any one from taking the law into their own hands? Anyone can become judge and executioner – not only the police and public officials. Anyone can form their own vigilante groups. There won't be any need for prisons or lawyers or judges. There won't be any peace, no order as long and human rights and the rule of law are disregarded. Meanwhile, the big criminals, the big thieves and murderers will continue to rule the land. If it is o.k. to kill criminals, who can prevent anyone from killing the biggest Criminal of them all? We could be entering another dark period of our history — like the dictatorial period in the past or worst.

(Posted by <u>Fr. Picx</u> at <u>5:57 PM</u>

ooOOoo

6.

My First Haircut in America

Fred Natividad

(My brief bio: In 1966 my wife, Francisca, and I immigrated from Pangasinan to Illinois where we worked and lived until we retired in 1988 and 1990 respectively. I was an accountant at the University of Illinois while Francisca was a nurse coordinator at Cook County Hospital in Chicago. After 35 years in Illinois we now live in Fredericksburg, Virginia, located 50 miles south of Washington DC. We celebrated our 50th anniversary (picture below in Amsterdam) recently with a trip to Europe instead of a big bash. Fred Natividad Posting from historic Virginia   =Say nanlapuan lingawen pian antay arapen. =Alamin ang pinang-galingan upang malaman ang paro-roonan. =Know where we had been to guide us where we are going. Fred Natividad, Livonia, Michigan © 2010, revised in Fredericksburg, VA © 2016.)

Dateline, Sept. 2016

One day in 1967, in Chicago, I went to a barbershop.

I recently arrived from the Philippines when the flood gates for immigrants from the Philippines opened up because of a new law that abolished immigration quotas from around the world. I read that in the past, in spite of the big joke of special relations between the Philippines and the United States, only 50 Filipinos were allowed to enter the United States annually.

Back to my haircut…

This was my first haircut in America and I was probably the first Filipino customer of the barber. Having just got off work, I was still in my suit and tie. I must have looked out of place among the blue collar types in the shop who probably did not expect this little brown skinned, slit eyed character from some unheard of country to be wearing a suit and tie.

"I need a haircut."

"Sure! Do you have money?"

Laughter from the other waiting customers.

After paying my bill I shelled out a five dollar bill tip. The barber was startled. Five dollars! I do not remember anymore the basic cost of a haircut in 1967 but I do remember the five dollar tip as quite enormous because the barber almost fainted. Heck, I was making the princely sum of four hundred fifty dollars a month when the prevailing blue collar minimum wage was maybe less than three dollars an hour. Also, I was used to making only the equivalent of less than a hundred U.S. dollars in Philippine pesos a month. Making four hundred fifty in America made me dizzyingly, if naively, magnanimous.

The blue collar crowd smirked. This tiny brown character in a suit and tie still proverbially smelled of the proverbial smelly immigration boats. In 1967 Filipinos were not as ubiquitous as they are in the 1990's. The barber shop was located in the mostly white neighborhood around Mt. Sinai Hospital in the vicinity of Ogden and California avenues. It is gone now.

In olden times the economy class in boats that ferried Europeans to Ellis Island probably smelled. Maybe to this blue collar crowd there was no reason to believe that boats from the Orient smelled any better. It so happened that, coincidentaly I did come to America by boat on the SS President Wilson. The blue collar crowd, of course, certainly did not have envision that my passage on the Wilson was in first class. They could not know that it was a farewell gift from my Manila employer.

On my next visit to the barber he announced to the other waiting customers that he must take care of me first because I called earlier for an appointment on this precise time of the day. He surprised me! He lied. I did not call for an appointment. I did not even know his phone number. Then he whispered: "You don't have to tip me with five dollars. You already made your point that you are not an Oriental version of a naive hillbilly.

He also whispered to me that he was a GI in MacArthur's liberation army in the Philippines in 1945 and the men he saw there were not tiny men in suits and ties but barefoot peasants.

If he was simply a patronizing s.o.b. I didn't mind. Heck, I enjoyed his extreme flattery.

ooOOoo

7.
The Last Autumn

Fred Natividad
@ Fred Natividad, Livonia, Michigan
Revised August 29, 2010
Fred Natividad Posting from historic Virginia   =Say nanlapuan lingawen pian antay arapen. =Alamin ang pinang-galingan upang malaman ang paro-roonan. =Know where we had been to guide us where we are going.

The sound of leaves in the neighborhood rustling to the rhythm of cool breezes of dying summer became more pronounced. Red, brown, and yellow leaves fluttered in slow abandon as they fell to the ground.

It was time for college again.

The boys - with their mother and her credit card - had done their final shopping. They bought enough new jeans and shirts and music tapes and whatever else. They did not buy any school supplies because they said they would buy what they would need at campus stores.

And so it was time - the annual trip 130 miles south of Winfield, Illinois, into deep corn and soybean country in the middle of which is located the sprawling flagship campus of the University of

Illinois that straddled the twin towns of Urbana and Champaign.

I had to give it to the boys. Our motor home served as their hauling truck They were able to cram into it incredible mountains of their stuff. Pots. Pans. A dorm fridge. A guitar. A boom box. Pair after pair of jeans. Sneakers. Jackets and sweaters with the orange logos of the University of Illinois. A typewriter. A computer...

And, yes, books. But not the kind of books of their academic disciplines.

I don't remember which of the boys volunteered to drive first. He nosed the groaning motor home out of the subdivision towards the country road that will lead to the ramp of the highway that will touch the outskirts of Champaign 130 miles down. They took turns driving, talking ceaselessly while munching potato chips and slurping pop. They didn't seem sentimental about the fact that this was their last trip to Champaign. This was their senior year.

The first thing Kikay did when we arrived at the dorm was to come up to their prearranged room. A Catholic outfit runs the dorm. Their room was already clean but Kikay, the perennial mother and housewife, insisted on dusting things before we brought up the stuff from the motor home. She insisted on arranging things in the room even if I told her that the boys will rearrange things their way anyway after we leave.

Then off we went to some Chinese restaurant for lunch, after which we drove the boys back to their dorm. We tarried as long as we could until it was really time for us to go home. The boys didn't seem to have any intention of hugging their mother goodbye. But Kikay did not feel any affront. She went to hug them with all kinds of trite advice that they have heard a thousand times. I went off and waited in the motorhome dreading the prospect of a three-hour drive back to Winfield without the boys taking turns at the wheel.

Dark came early, so it seemed, when we reached the house in Winfield. It was not a big house - it had only four bedrooms and its total square footage was only about 2,400. Yet it seemed so large when, as we entered, we switched the lights on. It was so empty. There were no college boys sprawled lazily in the living room watching some football game or some comedy sitcom.

Kikay quietly heated up some leftovers for our dinner. We ate in deafening silence. Our two boys were not around. For all we know at that very moment they were out at some college joint having some fun - or what to them was fun reacquainting with last year's classmates over beer and peanuts.

After dinner I opened my second can of beer and tried to watch TV in the living room. Kikay went upstairs. My mind, strangely, was not on the TV show that was on. I don't remember if it was a game show, or a comedy sitcom or a newscast.

Then I realized that Kikay was unusually quiet. Normally I could hear her nagging me about how loud the TV is. Or I could hear her tinkering with her pots and pans in the kitchen or stacking plates after removing them from the dishwasher. Perhaps she was doing her rosary beads but she usually did that before going to bed.

Curious, I went upstairs to find her leaning by the doorway of one bedroom staring at an empty bed. She was sobbing quietly. When I came up behind her she turned to face me and she led me wordlessly to the other room. Both rooms, of course, were empty. The beds were still unmade from last night. The boys didn't bother to fix their beds that morning.

Two semesters went fast. The boys graduated and they came home. But they did not come home in the context of really coming home. They merely came to use their beds as a way station. They were always out. Eventually they flew off the nest for good.

So it came to pass that we had to sell the house simply because it was too empty. We moved back to the city close to the first neighborhood we lived in when we first came to America. It has changed. We were told that it used to be a predominantly Italian neighborhood but now it has become populated with all kinds of ethnicities. We have moved a lot of times since then but every so often we think of that autumn evening when Kikay and I stared at our boys' empty, unmade beds in Winfield. We can't forget the last time the boys slept in their beds with any feeling of home.

We always remember our last autumn as a family.

ooOOoo

8.
A Night of Beer and Oysters
Fred Natividad

(Fred Natividad Posting from historic Virginia =Say nanlapuan lingawen pian antay arapen. =Alamin ang pinang-galingan upang malaman ang paro-roonan. =Know where we had been to guide us where we are going.)

Dateline, ©1974

Years ago we went on vacation by train to Florida. The ride was already part of our vacation with all the slow, leisurely views of scenery one does not enjoy on a plane thirty odd thousand feet up in the sky flying at about half a thousand miles per hour. And on the train the driving is left to the train engineer.

Scenery-wise traveling by car is comparable with the added advantage of being able to do impromptu stops at points of interest. That is if one is willing to drive especially if the trip is more than five hundred miles.

We visited a family in a navy housing compound in Mayport, Florida. Our host is my wife's brother, a navy man (a "squid" he calls himself) who was then assigned at the U.S. naval base there. While this was a family reunion it was also a visit to a naval base, a novel experience to us because back home we never had a chance to get inside the navy base at Subic Bay or the air base at Clark.

It turned out that besides a family reunion and a first time visit to a U.S. naval base we got into something we had not experienced before.

It was mid afternoon on our first day. We went shopping for dinner groceries, stopping at a nearby sea food store only to find oysters and mussels expensive enough for my brother in law to decide taking us to some beach. Oysters and mussels there are free for the taking. So armed with pails and a pair of shovels, we drove a few miles out of the base and headed to a ferry that took us to a sandy beach of some river. The tide was low and the beach was wide open. We did not have to wade into the water.

We enjoyed the unique thrill of gathering mussels and oysters. We dug up the sand for mussels that clung to the roots of beach vegetation. It took some doing to free the mussels from their host plants. They clung tightly with their beards around their host plants as if they knew that once harvested they wind up getting boiled for dinner. Indeed we had mussels for dinner that evening. No oysters for dinner - more on that later.

At the sight of so many oysters exposed on the beach not attached to poles in the water as I thought they would be I excitedly picked up every oyster within reach. My brother in law laughed at my excitement and suggested that I just pick up the larger ones. With an embarrassed chagrin I put the small ones back on the sand.

On the way home we picked up two six-packs of beer, a bottle of hot sauce, and another bottle of lemon juice. For dinner, our wives, using an old country recipe, boiled some mussels in ginger, onions, freshly ground black pepper and tomatoes. The mussel broth served as our soup. On purpose we ignored the oysters we brought home.

We had something more delicious in mind. After our light dinner my brother in law and I began the fun. Shucking oysters open with dull screw drivers we seasoned the delicious morsels with hot sauce and lemon juice and then gleefully slurped them out of the shell. At the time we were then young and relatively healthy. We had no diet restrictions nor were we concerned about imbibing too much beer. Our tummies were not unsightly bulges then.

We slurped oysters and drank beer until late that evening. The kids got tired watching us. They went to bed, obviously puzzled at what's so exciting about slimy mollusks. Our wives tried a few oysters but they did not last into the night like we did. Fortunately we did not suffer any tummy aches. However, we did suffer some hang over next morning but not badly enough that we were able to take the children swimming. The lifeguards were navy noncoms, one of whom was a friend of my brother in law.

Confident that the children are under the care of the U.S. Navy we left them while we went around touring the base. As a civilian only aware of the navy from a distance I noticed here the old saying that the military is not a democracy. There is a training-based culture of caste system. We passed by a recreation center and I asked my brother in law if we can have a drink there. He said no because that place is for noncoms below his rating. We passed another one and he said we can't go there either because it is for commissioned officers.

He pointed out a ship that was a floating machine shop where one of the officers was a

Filipino. Filipino "squids" have come a long way. They are no longer confined to mess duties or shoe shine boys for officers. My brother in law, like other Filipino boys recruited at Cavite, started his navy career as a mess steward. He has come up as a Chief (E7) and when he retired after 30 years he was a Master Chief (E9).

We decided that evening to go back to our oysters at home. We had only a few oysters and a beer each this time. We did not want to suffer a hangover in the morning because we will be driving the kids to Epcot.

oo0Ooo

9.
Healing & Killing

Sen. Rene Sagisag
(Saguisag & Associates Lawyers
4045 Bigasan Street, Palanan,1235 Makati
Office Nos. (+632) 551-6350/833- 4140
Fax No. (+632) 831-2276)
(ravslaw@gmail.com)

Dateline, Sept. 21, 2016, WFA Group

It is plain wrong to mark September 21, 1972 as the notorious Day of Infamy. For me it was just another day in the office.

As head of the San Beda Free Legal Aid Clinic, I monitored from my Mendiola office a rally in Plaza Miranda, that Thursday, just in case I'd need to rush over. Ka Pepe Diokno, Charito Planas, Bal Pinguel, et al.. spoke. September 22, Friday, ho-hum, again, save that on my way home that night from San Beda, to our rented Sandejas, Pasay apartment, my Beetle radio announced the spurious ambush of Manong Johnny Ponce Enrile, who admitted the falsehood on February 22, 1986.

44 Septembers ago, when Macoy inflicted martial law, the following describes how I felt as an uhugin lawyer and saw other Panyeros/as like -

"The German lawyer [who] was . . .particularly prepared to accept as `law' anything that called itself by that name, was printed at government expense and seemed to come `von oben herab." L. Fuller, Positivism and Fidelity to Law - A Reply to Professor Hart, 71 Harv. L. Rev. 630, 659 (1958). "Hitler did not come to power by a violent revolution. .

The exploitation of legal forms started cautiously and became bolder as power was consolidated. The first attacks on the established order were on ramparts which, if they were manned by anyone, were manned by lawyers and judges. These ramparts fell almost without a struggle." Id.

Tañada, Diokno, Salonga, Ordoñez, Garchitorena, Arroyo, Gonzalez (Raul), Bobbit Sanchez, et al. were grossly outnumbered by the Fil-German types, as the ramparts fell with little struggle. So newbies such as the Jojo Binays, Odie Melchors, By Bocars, Ed Araullos, Boy Ellas, Jimmy Malanyaons, Jun Factorans, Boyet Fernandezes, Hessie Mallilins, and a few others, including myself, tried to fill in the breach. Macoy failed to heed the advice in Shakespeare's Henry

VI on what take-over plotters should do: "The first thing we do, let's kill all the lawyers," in supreme tribute to those who would ask the foolish questions of the day, and hang the costs and consequences, and not let the ramparts fall without any struggle. (Of course St. Ives was a lawyer and yet became a saint, and the people were astonished.)

Ka Pepe organized the Free Legal Assistance Group (FLAG), after being detained from 1972 to 1974 without being charged! I joined. In 1980, some of us who thought lawyers should take public stands aside from traditional lawyering, formed MABINI (Movement of Attorneys for Brotherhood, Integrity and Nationalism, Inc.) but kept our warm ties with FLAG and iconic Ka Pepe. I am among the relics and antiques left, MD, Masamang Damo, marching again to the beat of a different drummer (Thoreau), taking the less travelled road (Frost), sailing against the wind (the Kennedys), and asking "why not?" while seeing things that never were (others may ask "why" , seeing things that are - GB Shaw).

We are now forming a new group, with new blood, while we watch what the quiet Integrated Bar of the Philippines, the Philippine Bar Association, the Philconsa, the big bufetes, and others will do in the wake of the extrajudicial executions far exceeding what happened in late 1972. Population reduced violently by 3,000 in weeks!

In the late 80's we were delighted to gain vocal support from interlopers Prez Jimmy Carter, State Asec Patricia Derian, Amnesty International, atbp. Pakialameros/ as.

In 1986, alien interference was capped by divine intervention. The world was shocked and awed by People Power, which saw the nearly bloodless end of the reign of a kleptocratic gross human rights violator who Digong idolizes and would now want him to rest with heroes. Digong should consult FVR, who the Marcoses put one over on, in 1993.

I am on the side of fellow Bedan Leila de Lima against fellow Bedans Vit Aguirre (our hardworking colleague in the case of Hubert Webb) and Digong Duterte (with whose courageous principled Mom I marched in Davao after Ninoy was salvaged). I was flabbergasted to see Vit acting like the Speaker or Committee Chair of the House he seemed to own last Tuesday. Usually, outside counsel is not much more than part of the furniture, while the elected lawmakers dominate and scintillate.

Of course litigators walk through with their witnesses on their testimony. And no lawyer should ask a question the answer to which he doesn't already know, particularly on cross. Trial Technique 101.

Speaker Bebot Alvarez, who may or may not remember me, is sounding like a Certified Tuta.

Vit and Digong should stop naming and shaming people and instead just file cases against them, particularly the wealthy and well-connected. Not enough to increase the body count of the poorest of the poor who should be rehabbed, with better planning. Packed prisons depress and convert humans into brutes.

I am comfy with underdogs. Sen. Dick Gordon took ousted Lei's place. I trust him if only cuz ang hambog galit sa kapwa hambog. He can stand up to Digs, on principle. When Erap kicked Dick around so needlessly in 1998, I assisted him against my Canvassing client Erap. Dick told me that some Jesuit taught him that "in this world, the world laughs with you but, you weep alone." As a human being, Christian and lawyer, I say, "if you need me and you have no one else, you'll never walk and weep alone. I'll walk and weep with you, if you will allow me." When Erap fell from overdog to underdog, I finally heeded his request to join his legal team. I walked and wept with him, along with his friends and wives. I entered my appearance and joined his formidable battery but an accused goes to bat with two strikes against him. Like beleaguered Sen. Leila. Hang in there, Lei! I admire your moral stamina. Let's see what Vit will do with the names you supplied as elements of the alleged Davao Death Squad.

There is no substitute for due process and no hardline bloody policy has succeeded anywhere in the world. If there is money to be made, the failed drug policy won't erase trafficking in which Dona Josefa Marcos engaged while teaching in Arellano High School, and arrested by top cop Telesforo Tenorio, according to Tibo Mijares in the Conjugal Dictatorship. Tibo disappeared while his teenaged son, Boyet, was sadistically salvaged.

I see a ray of hope in Imee's seeking forgiveness for his Pop's abuses and am appalled by Bongbong' s insult of the human rights victims as only after money. No wonder, poor unknown Leni G. Robredo beat him, and fellow Bicolanos Alan (by marriage), Chiz, Gringo and Sonny, splitting the votes with the Oragons while billionaire

BB had his Solid North. Feisty Leila is also Bicolana.

The voters could have chosen a Healing Prez. But a plurality preferred a Killing One, who gives the rich due process but spares few in unkind naming and shaming. Traffic, after 80 days of Digong is much worse in Metro Manila. What if he and Bato de la Rosa execute ten "resisting&quo t; scofflaw drivers? A remedy worse than the disease.

Sec. Vit Aguirre can just file charges, if he has the evidence, against Lei and others named and shamed. He should recall how our common client, Hubert Webb, was named and shamed, tried and convicted by publicity, early on, and spent more than 15 years in jail for something I then said I'd carry to my grave he did not commit. He was thousands of miles away but the hooting throng carried the day.

Obsta principiis. Resist the first encroachments.

Oh, yes, kudos to Ted Locsin, who may share with Digong a liking for the dirty finger sign, but the communications guys can always explain they only mean to say, "you are No. 1." The spin I gave in 1986., if my memory is true.

ooO0Ooo

10.

Duterte and Our Nation's Health

Philip S. Chua MD, FACS, FPCS

(The author, a Cardiac Surgeon Emeritus in Northwest Indiana and Las Vegas, is chairman of the Filipino United Network – USA, a 501(c)3 United States humanitarian and anti-graft Foundation, and a weekly columnists of Cebu Daily News, MALAYA Philippine national daily, and six Fil-Am newspapers in the United States. Visit philipSchua.com   Email: scalpelpen@gmail.com)

Dateline, Sept. 2016, Global Balita

With the election of Rodrigo Duterte, The Punisher and Dirty Harry of Davao, as the next president of the Philippines, are the Filipinos headed towards a healthier, safer, and corruption-free nation?

This is most certainly a tall order, which realistically could take decades to accomplish, but The Punisher promised he would achieve this much sooner…"in six months." Obviously, the voters believed him.

The PNoy Aquino administration has impressively initiated an earnest battle against graft and corruption with his Daang Matuwid theme, sending his predecessor, former president Gloria Arroyo, charged with plunder, to hospital arrest, hopefully to jail soon, dethroning Supreme Court Chief Justice Renato Corona, for failure to file his SALN and unexplained wealth, and sending to jail Senate President Juan Ponce Enrile, Senators Jinggoy Estrada and Bong Revilla plus dozens of other indicted politicians, awaiting trial. The PNoy administration has been fighting a deeply-entrenched, decades-old, massive culture of graft and corruption pervasive in the government, and history will credit him for his genuine valiant endeavors against all odds during his 6-year term.

Unfortunately, Enrile was released by some members of the Supreme Court "because he was old and frail," a misplaced compassion to which I had taken exception in my previous column, where I countered that "if Enrile was not too old and frail to commit plunder he should not be too old to go to jail for this most vicious crime against our country, a crime whose penalty was death under our previous Constitution." This was, indeed, a travesty of justice.

President-elect Duterte also wants to bring back death penalty. While death penalty will not totally eliminate plunder and other ferocious crimes, it certainly could act as a deterrent. When convicted corrupt leaders in some Asian countries are executed by a firing squad in a public square, which we, a "compassionate and forgiving Christian nation" describe as "barbaric," corruption in those countries has been minimized. So, are we really not more "barbaric" when we allow plunderers to ruin our nation, its integrity, and its marginalized people and get unpunished?

Do you think any of our government officials would even think of committing plunder if the penalty was death, and the sentence carried out expeditiously? This is a vicious crime, and as Deterte stated, we must be brutal when we fight corrupt officials and those dealing in drug. His phenomenal election is a clear mandate for him to be brutal in cleansing the nation of plunderers, drug dealers, corrupt policemen and military, and all other criminals, and equally ruthless in eliminating poverty in the Philippines where more than a third of the people are homeless and hungry, courtesy of these criminals with deep pockets walking in the halls of Congress and all the way to the bank.

If Duterte is sincere and true to his promises, his first act should be to declare no presidential pardon for Arroyo, Corona, Enrile, Jinggoy Estrada, Bong Revilla, and all other officials already in jail, when they are proven guilty. Let's see what he does with the Binay family and other officials on his List. Let's see if The Punisher will honor our constitution and strictly implement our penal codes, with justice for all.

Since we claim to be a nation of laws, we must not allow anybody to be above the law. If government officials, who must justifiably be held to a higher standard, commit the crime of plunder or any crime, they must be treated like common criminals and dealt with even more severely. They did not have compassion for our poor people languishing in the gutter of poverty and for our devastated nation, who are really the collateral victims of their greed, so these plunderers deserve no compassion at all from our legal system or from We, The People.

Hopefully, The Punisher will eliminate all the extravagant amenities elite prisoners currently enjoy in jail, like larger cells, with special beds and furniture, air-conditioning, televisions, microwave, computers, a mini-gym for exercise, etc. in their own cell, where they even hold "bonga" parties at their leisure. All these cost the tax payers hundreds of millions a year, money that could help alleviate poverty instead. The jail cell must be a punishment (not a reward) for criminals, not a house of luxury. They must be provided a jail cell with a bed, a fan, light, ordinary toilet facilities, and reading materials, like what other criminals (with lesser offense) get in stricter countries. These VIP plunderers deserve Papillon and not the Ritz Carlton or even Hotel Sogo.

The jail administrators and officials who had allowed this insult to our justice system and the loss of perhaps billions of pesos over the years from the federal coffers happen, must all be indicted and charged accordingly, and if found guilty, and not only fired, but jailed themselves.

Our president-elect also plans to make the Philippines a smoke-free nation. Smokers are spraying the air with second-hand poison smoke which is even more toxic, causing respiratory tract infection, emphysema, chronic obstructive lung disease, heart disease, and cancers. Indeed, the public should not be forced to inhale carcinogen-polluted air. Human rights for the few must be second only to majority rights and national health.

Duterte's surprising phenomenal victory symbolizes the people's impatient desire to eliminate graft and corruption among our government officials, military, policemen, and drug dealers and common criminals in our society. Well-informed Filipinos are simply fed up.

The people have spoken clearly and loudly. The Punisher has been elected. Let's give Duterte his due to cleanse the nation in his own unconventional way, like what he did for Davao, which has been a more peaceful, healthier, and safer place for law-abiding citizens since he was elected mayor. Plunder, drug dealing, kurakot, and other crimes will not stop until the plunderers, drug dealers, and the common criminals are eliminated or jailed for good.

When we consider Dirty Harry's "modus operandi," let us remember with compassion the more than 30 million fellow Filipinos who are homeless and hungry, who, together with their children go to bed at night, not only with empty stomach but with empty dreams and a nightmare for a future. Let us not forget the shame we, Filipinos, face being notorious as the world's most corrupt nation, a laughing stock of the global community.

If Duterte could save our nation by eliminating the plunderers, drug dealers, and other criminals, and rebuild the Philippine society, let him be severely brutal against all criminals **proven guilty**. And that is the only boundary We, The People, should set for him as he metes out justice, if we sincerely love and want to save our suffering fellowmen and demoralized nation, and gain the respect of the world.

We must all either put up, or shut up and give Duterte a chance to do his job freely and judge him later about his positive accomplishments, or lack thereof, for our beloved Philippines. We owe him, the people's choice, at least that much.

ooo00oo

11.
Drugs can destroy a nation

Philip S. Chua MD, FACS, FPCS

Dateline, Sept. 5, 2016, Heart To Heart Column

The illegal drug problem here and abroad is not a modern crisis. Almost 3 centuries ago, an illegal drug brought down an empire, the Imperial China. If not drastically eliminated, illegal drug trafficking and use, a massive cancer in the Philippines, could destroy our nation. Indeed, President Rodrigo Duterte's aggressive war on drugs is most welcome, a brutal and desperate solution to a brutal and desperate situation.

China, in 1793, was rich in history and had a sophisticated culture. It invented kites, movable type, and gun powder, and perfected the production of tea, silk, and porcelain. In 1825, the British introduced opium to China and soon the Chinese became addicted to the drug. An illegal trade quickly developed in spite of the Emperor's prohibition. Some of the government officials, leading businessmen, and a vast number of Chinese were hooked on this drug. Weakened by this societal cancer, the Chinese government, unable to protect its own people, lost the support of the nation. Less than a century later, the empire was dead.

OPLAN: TOKHANG

President Duterte's earnest zero-tolerance policy on illegal drugs is what our poor country needs. With about 30 percent of Filipinos languishing in the gutter of poverty, who are homeless and hungry, who go to bed at night, not only with empty stomach, but with empty dreams, and who wake up, day after day, to a bleak tomorrow, we cannot afford to allow illegal drug trafficking in this country.

Knowing the evils of drug trafficking and use, President Duterte has waged a massive, bold, and aggressive war (Oplan Tokhang: "Approach and Talk") against drug lords, dealers, and users, with the equally determined PNP Chief General "Bato" Ronald M. dela Rosa, the "Rock,"as his prime front-liner.

More than 600,000 drug addicts have voluntarily surrendered within the fist two months of Duterte's presidency. As of August 31, 2016, 929 drug dealer suspects have been killed in encounters with the police and another 1,507 by unknown attackers, which are being investigated. Ten police officers have been killed during the various stings. So far, the total fatalities reported: at least 2,448. The results of the anti-drug campaign have been very impressive, considering the new administration has been in office for barely five months.

The many deaths attributed to the government's war on drugs have been labeled by some quarters as extra-judicial killings, "without due process." Whether vigilantes were responsible for the summary executions, no one seems to be sure. Many of these killings were done by tandem motorbike riders on the fly.

Instead of convicting the President of "EJK" right off the bat, on the basis of innuendoes and his big mouth and his bold pronouncements, perhaps he should also be accorded due process first. Let's have all the evidence in. When he is found guilty beyond reasonable doubt, that is the time for us, We, The People, to condemn him. But not before.

Due Process

There are two kinds of due process provided by the Philippine Constitution: (1) Substantive, "which requires the intrinsic validity of the law in interfering with the rights of the person to life, liberty or property. In short, it is to determine whether *it has a valid governmental objective like for the interest of the public* as against mere particular class," and (2) Procedural, one which hears before it condemns."

Removing all our personal biases on this issue for a moment, let us analyze the realities of the matter in a poor country such as ours. Let us take the example of a drug lord or a dealer, well known in their Barangay for their usual open illegal business, catering drugs to the local residents.

One of the objectives of due process is to be certain, beyond reasonable doubt, that the accused is guilty or innocent. In most towns, the residents know who the drug lord or dealers are for decades.

Now, if a vigilante kills a known drug lord or dealer, the killing is extrajudicial, because there was "no procedural due process," but is there a substantive due process "for public interest," in this case?

But let us go through the motion of due process as human rights advocates (of which I am one) demand. Since the courts are already overloaded, it would take months, if not a year or so, to adjudicate the case. And there could be more than 2 million drug offenders. Our jails are already crowded. We need more prisons. More funds.

While in jail, the drug lord or dealer will be provided free board and lodging with air-conditioning, medical care, exercise and recreational activities, television, etc. And it is public knowledge that bongga parties have been held in jail and even call girls are available for inmates who have the connection.

Whether you realize it or not, you and I will be subsidizing and financing all of the above with the tax money we pay each year, funds which could be channeled to house, feed, and provide medical care and education for the poor and their suffering families.

Are we, who are demanding due process, myself included, willing to contribute more to our government in order to build more jails to house, feed, and provide for the drug lords and dealers while in prison (without having to take the budget from the DSW, DOH, DOE, DOD, etc., for this purpose)?

The annual expense per inmate is P73,910, almost 3 times the P23,775 spent by the Department of Education for the basic education of a student. The combined budget of "almost P2.5 billion for 135,000 inmates is larger than the P4.27 billion the Department of Social Welfare spends to feed 2.1 million undernourished children a year."

The almost P74,000 expense per inmate per year does not even include the expenses to be incurred (budget for) the police, government prosecutors, and public legal defense provided for each indigent defendant.

When the drug lord shoots back and is killed in an encounter with the police, the government saves at least P73,910 per person per year, and multiplied by at least 2 million offenders, the savings could be a truly significant amount. Those inmates will be in prison for a number of years. And the expenses will continue to add up, like a taxi meter. These savings could well help alleviate poverty, improve our education and national healthcare, and fund infrastructure projects around the country.

In spite of these realities and expensive complexity of the law, to the disadvantage and detriment of the poorest of the poor in the

Philippines, the application of due process must be honored and extrajudicial killings must nonetheless be outlawed.

In the same token, let's have all the facts before we judge anyone. Least President Duterte, the People's Choice, still with 91% public approval rating today, who has a noble dream of a drug-free Philippines and a greater nation and who is putting his life on the line to save our country from corruption, poverty, chaos, and destruction.

Isn't this, after all, the essence of due process?

ooOOoo

12.

A travesty of justice

Philip S. Chua, MD, FACS, FPCS

Dateline, July 21, 2014, Heart To Heart Column

Now that the three musketeers of the pork barrel scam, and their mastermind Muse and Cheerleader Janet Napoles, are behind bars, and all the rest of their fellow (35 or so) plunderers or conspirators soon joining them, another deviant facet of our Philippine culture, besides the culture of corruption, has started to emerge and come under the spotlight once again. I am referring to the government's and some people's warped sense of justice and fairness in dealing with criminals in jail.

The jail cells for these criminals have been refurbished with our taxes, the people's money, specifically to make their incarceration less uncomfortable. Why the special treatment for these legislator law breakers? Instead of spending the funds for the reconstruction, it should have been given to the homeless and the hungry, and for the schooling of those children in poverty.

Bong, who has been most arrogant, hostile, contentious, and bellicose of all, has been complaining of rats in his jail cell. There is nothing wrong with that. Rats belong to where rats are. Besides, the more than 30 percent of Filipinos in the gutter of poverty today might even gladly take the place of these jailed legislators, with free air-conditioned shelter, with security guards, free TV, free food, and free medical care, etc. And special amenities to boot.

Jails are for criminals and criminals must be in jail. That's what our constitution and penal code state. There is no provision in either of those two which states that plunderers who are VIPs, celebrities, or legislators, or even a former president of the country, proven guilty of their crime, should be accorded a special treatment, housed in a Hilton, or even a cheap pension house, version of a jail, and allowed to have amenities like a TV in their cell, special beds, microwave oven, etc., and to party and receive visitors all they want. Criminals are jailed to suffer and pay their debt to society.

The plunderers and those yet to be indicted in the public sector corruption have caused our government and tax payers about P250 Billion annually. That massive hemorrhage from the national coffers could have provided more than one million new homes for the homeless, 523 classrooms, feeding more than 7 million hungry people, rehabilitation of more than 5.5 million hectares of damaged farmlands, medical care for 210 million indigent families, purchase of more than 94,000 ambulances, 12,500 fire trucks, 400,000 non-polluting electronic jeepneys, more than 17 million school computers, 50 million scholarship programs from the Commission on Higher Education, all for our people, especially those in the gutter of poverty, the very direct victims of these plunderers, led by Enrile, Bong Revilla and Jinggoy Estrada.

Common criminals in jail for stealing food or money for care of their sick family members or for education of their children are the ones we should show understanding and compassion, and give special treatment to, if at all, compared to these plunderers.

Legislators and all government officials or employees, like those in high offices, Supreme Court, members of Congress, priests, policemen and others in law enforcement offices, and other public servants, must be treated to a higher standard.

A priest raping someone is worst than a common rapist; a policeman, justice of the supreme court, or members of congress, who steal commit a graver crime than non-official thieves. These criminals must be held fully accountable for their crimes, and not be rewarded with VIP treatments compared to those others in jail. The maximum penalty required by law must be meted to them, without mercy. They did not show mercy to our suffering, disenfranchised, people now wallowing in abject poverty, with their nose barely above water.

Why should Enrile be shown extra mercy, or Bong and Jinggoy given special care? We must respect and follow our laws, our penal code. They must be housed and fed, and not be abused in jail. If they are legitimately ill, they must, like other prisoners, be given medical care in jail, or, be hospitalized, if medical justified. They must be treated like other criminals in jail. No special treatment. The jailed criminal must suffer the consequences of their act. Of all people, Enrile, the framer of the Marcos Martial Law, and legislators Bong and Jinggoy, ought to know. They knowingly and with premeditation, violated the law, now they must suffer for that.

If the government wants to give special amenities (TV, cushion, cellphone, microwave oven, etc.,) it must also give the same benefits to all the other prisoners in all jails in the country, without exception.

As a cardiovascular surgeon, I know that the common irregular heart beat is not a justifiable reason for Gigi Reyes not to be in jail or for her to be in a hospital, like Gloria Arroyo, whose condition does not really require hospitalization. There are hundreds of millions of people round the world active and working normally with the common irregular heart beat or neck arthritis and pain. Only life-threatening medical and surgical conditions should be accepted as an indication for hospitalization, which is standard practice in the medical community around the world. Our justice system is being abused by these medical excuses to stay out of jail, and our government seems to be falling for it.

Physicians who certify that such and other trivial medical condition are excuses to be out of jail, or require hospitalization, when proven wrong by our Department of Health or reputable medical societies, must themselves be brought to court and jailed. These physicians are then, as corrupt as those plunderers they are trying to shield from justice.

When former president Gloria Arroyo, while in office, now in hospital arrest herself for plunder, etc., pardoned Erap Estrada, who was jailed for plunder, she irreparably damaged our justice system and the reputation of the Philippines in the eyes of the international community, who has branded the Philippines as a most corrupt country.

In some countries, who we, a democratic and basically a Catholic nation, call barbaric and unchristian for speedy trials and public executions of plunderers among their officials, graft and corruption is rarer, compared to the Philippines, where VIP plunderers and murderers could escape the justice system.

Are we really more democratic, more Christian, when we turn our cheek the other way and allow the plunderers in our government to proliferate and continue decades after decades to rob the nation's coffers, people's tax money at the expense of those millions in poverty and the countless victims of the various natural disasters, and when the plunderers are caught, give them pardon and allow them to run for public office again?

Why are we so stupid and masochistic? Why do we have that self-destruct culture in us? We are an intelligent people, so why can We, the People, not be a united majority and condemn these plunderers to the maximum penalty, without mercy, and simply abide by the penal code of the nation?

If Christ did not turn His cheek the other way and aggressively condemned usury and the evils that went with it during His time, you can imagine how He would treat these plunderers in our midst today.

I say, we, Filipinos, as a nation, are more unchristian, less compassionate, more barbaric to our nation and its people to be soft on plunderers, compared to those nations who expeditiously kill in public squares the massively guilty few to protect the greater majority, especially their marginalized poor.

Besides putting the plunderers behind bars for life (reclusion perpetua), the government must take back the total amount these legislators stole and confiscate their properties and other assets as a payment of the penalty to the amount prescribed by law. All these billions of pesos could then be used to ameliorate poverty in the country.

These corrupt legislators and their co-conspirators need a painful lesson. Let's give them one, with maximum pain. *(Please visit philipSchua.com)*

ooOOoo

13.
Are We, Humans, Really Civilized?
(Or, are we for the birds?)

Philip S. Chua, MD, FACS, FPCS

Dateline, Timeless, Heart To Heart Column

I was driving to work one early morning a few years ago in Munster, Indiana, when I noticed a flock of Canada geese flying against a beautiful backdrop of a golden orange rising sun that was eagerly peering over the clear horizon. The picturesque scene became even more poignant when I observed that the geese were flying in a perfect reversed V-formation. One seemed to be the leader of the pack, at the very apex, and the rest, in an orderly fashion followed in a reversed V-formation. At one point, another goose flew ahead and assumed the "leadership" at the apex of the V. When the "leader" got tired, another flew to the apex, the former "leader" went behind the flank. They seemed to each take turn. Everything was smooth and easy flying, and quite orderly.

The reason came back to me as I recalled a book I once read. Birds, in general, have the instinct to know that the wind they fly against offers most aerodynamic resistance if they fly alone or on a straight frontal line. Flying in a reversed V-formation, with the apex cutting through the headwind, makes it a lot easier for the others behind to fly. The "leader" at the apex gets the most wind resistance, and less and lesser for those behind, who are covered by the birds in front of them. The leader, as in our daily life, takes the greatest burden, the grave responsibility, to serve and protect his "constituents." And all of this appears to take place in an organized fashion, with no hesitation, no delays, no bickering, no pushing, no wrangling, as if each bird knew precisely its individual role and was graciously compliant.

How I wish we, humans, self-proclaimed the most civilize and most intelligent of all creatures on the planet earth, would be as "civilize, compassionate, considerate, and orderly"` as these birds. Imagine how wonderful it would be if we, brothers and sisters of the world, would stop fighting, hurting, destroying and killing each other, and instead, understand, accept, help and protect each other like these flying creatures of God.

It is not too late. Perhaps We, the People, could initiate spreading love, compassion, and understanding to all our fellow men the world over, of any race, color, creed, religion, status in life, and gender, while we have time, sanity, and wisdom.

Obviously, the transformation will not be easy, as the history of man has so far shown us. But human beings better start soon, even a little bit each year or each decade, before we unwittingly blow each other up, together with Mother Earth, into shameful particles, bits and pieces, of historical ashes in the galaxy. The only legacy our specie would leave behind then would be our Homo Sapiens stupidity.

ooOOoo

14.

Why I Publish and/or Reprint Books And Why My Service is Free?

By Tatay Jobo Elizes, Self-Publisher

Writings are timeless and they act as mirrors of history. I publish writings as they remain relevant anytimeThere are also writers who write a lot but never publish them. There are also old books with no more prints available. The solution is to publish/reprint.

I am offering these services free of charge because of the availability of print-books-on-demand (POD) system nowadays. I can produce the book, but the prints are not free.

Why put your writings in a book? And not just in the internet? I recommend that writings be retained in a hard copy or in book form or printed form for posterity. The book will always be there among your collections or libraries. Not all use the internet. The internet access has its technical problems. Writings in the internet may be erased erroneously. Free storage is hard to access. Paid storage may be returned or lost.

For those looking for a publisher, especially if you have a novel or many essays, I can produce the paperback book under your own authorship at no cost. I can produce art books, family tree books, family albums/pictorials, biographies, joke books, song hits books, travelogues, reunions, color or black & white, etc.

Please buy online as paperback or kindle at **http://tinyurl.com/mj76ccq** (copy and paste to your browser). Permission had been granted by the author/ authors to print their books under my free self-publishing service. They own copyrights to their works. Interested reader may request free reading of any of my books, articles or essays via online reading or ebook. Just email me: **job_elizes@yahoo.com** My Books Catalog can be seen at **www.jobelizes6.wix.com/mysite**. The catalogue will grow as years pass by because of additional titles to be published. I continue to publish or reprint books as a means to archive them in hard copy and/or digital form, for posterity and legacy. Thank you.

oo0Ooo